# Hemingway's GUNS

Silvio Calabi, Steve Helsley, Roger Sanger

A SHOOTING SPORTSMAN BOOK

www.shootingsportsman.com

Copyright © 2010 by
Silvio Calabi, Steve Helsley and Roger Sanger
Photographs copyright as credited
All rights reserved

ISBN 978-0-89272-720-9

Designed by Lynda H. Mills

Printed in the United States

5      4      3      2      1

Library of Congress Cataloging-in-Publication Information
available on request

A SHOOTING
SPORTSMAN
BOOK
www.shootingsportsman.com

Distributed to the trade by National Book Network

# TABLE OF CONTENTS

Acknowledgements ................................................................3

Introduction ....................................................................5

A Firearms Vocabulary ..........................................................10

The Model 12 Pumpguns .........................................................13

The Browning Superposed .......................................................23

Two Browning Automatic 5s .....................................................33

The Winchester Model 21 Shotguns ..............................................38

A Pair of Merkel Over/Unders & a Single .......................................50

The Beretta S3 Over/Under .....................................................60

The Griffin & Howe .30-06 Springfield .........................................68

Mannlicher-Schoenauer Rifles ..................................................82

The .577 Nitro Express & Other Double Rifles ..................................93

Three (Four?) Colt Woodsman Pistols ..........................................109

The Model 61 Winchester & Other .22 Rifles ...................................121

A Thompson Submachine Gun ....................................................130

A Big-Bore Mauser, or Two ....................................................134

The W. & C. Scott & Son Pigeon Gun ...........................................140

Various: Adamy, Darne, Sarasqueta, Arrizabalaga, 'Alba' ......................154

Citations ....................................................................166

Bibliography .................................................................169

Index ........................................................................174

# WITH GRATITUDE

Many people helped in the creation of this book. The authors wish in particular to thank Dr. Miriam Mandel of the Dept. of English and American Studies at Tel Aviv University; Ian Parker of Nairobi; Griffin & Howe historian Bob Beach; Aaron Edward Hotchner, who prefers to be known as Hotch; and Patrick Hemingway. The late Lloyd Arnold, photographer, author and member of the tribe, deserves great thanks for taking a hunter's interest in his friend Ernest's guns. And we are beholden to Sue, Marilyn and Kathy for listening patiently to several lifetimes' worth of EH stories.

Others who provided material assistance (we can only hope the list is complete) include: Terry Allen, Edith Amsterdam, Dietrich Apel, Johnny Artymovich, Don Atkinson, Susan Beegel, Cav. Ugo Gussalli Beretta, Shannon Besoyan, Guy Bignell, Guy Bonnivier, Allen Brooks, Shari Buchanan, Sonja Calabi, Sean Campbell, Paul Carella, Larry Carter, Paul Chapman, Dr. Kirk Curnutt, Michael DeChevrieux, Tom Donoghue, Axel Eichendorff, Mike Engster, Tim Gardiner, Dr. Margaret Greeley, Tom Gresham, Maryrose Grossman, Graham Halsey, Gloria Gunter, Valerie Danby-Smith Hemingway, Ron Hickman, Einar Hoff, Sandra Hofferber, Will Hoiles, Peter Horn, Bob Hunter, Jim Julia, Mark A. Keefe IV, Andy Kent, Sue Kerfoot, James King, Dieter Krieghoff, Roger Lake, Sean Larkin, Charles Lee, Roxie Theisen Livingston, Forrest MacMullen, Lynda Mills, Warren Newman, John Nodop, Lisa Oakes, Dr. Bruce Patterson, Michael Petrov, Joseph Plummer, Bud Purdy, Nick Purdy, Patrick Quinn, Mike Riedel, Ned Schwing, Rob Shelton, Sam Smallidge, Bill Smallwood, Lorraine Smario, Jon Speed, Michael Steere, Ralph Stuart, Mike Stumbo, Bruce Tebbe, Laurence Thomson, Anthony Tregear, David Trevallion, Catherine Trippett, Andrey Ugarov, Chuck Webb, Elke Weiss, Ron D. White, Larry Wilson, Lee Witten, Greg Woods, Kevin Woods, Susan Wrynn, Michael Wysocki, Lydia Zelaya.

The most memorable writing in this book comes from Ernest Hemingway himself, from:

John F. Kennedy Library

# INTRODUCTION

## HEMINGWAY THE HUNTER

This book grew out of one Hemingway sentence, a seemingly casual but obviously rich aside in *Under Kilimanjaro*, a book about an African safari:

"The Purdey was not a Purdey but a straight-stocked long-barreled Scott live-pigeon full choke in both barrels that I had bought from a lot of shotguns a dealer had brought down from Udine to the Kechlers' villa in Codroipo."

Unraveling these 40 words plunged us into Hemingway's life and identity, the things he poured into his writing.

Two generations before the modern techno-thriller novel, Ernest Hemingway the storyteller knew that detail conferred credibility. Not so much detail that it swamped his narrative, but enough that we understood that he understood: This is how one hooks up a billfish. This is how a partisan blows a bridge. This is what a series of *verónicas* does to a fighting bull. This is why a gunstock must not be too long. Hemingway never wrote about anything until he had lived it, inhaled it, slept on it and dipped his fingers in its blood, sometimes literally. Then, when it was time to put words on paper, he did not indulge in tedious explanation of technical details, whether it was a Swahili expression or the difference between a hit with a softnose and a solid bul-

let. *You've got to keep up*, he seems to be saying to his readers; *it's worth it*. Or: *You don't get it? Don't worry, I do. Just pay attention to the story!*

Ernest Hemingway was a journalist and a novelist, but not just an observer; he could make the story and he could be the story. He had the power to affect events and lives directly, not just through his words. And everywhere he collected trophies—extraordinary friends, fantastic experiences, great gamefish and animals. With his typewriter and his fishing boat and his guns, Hemingway was always a hunter.

Born outside Chicago in 1899, Hemingway grew up in an era when even urban Americans still had an easy familiarity with firearms. The West had just been pacified, but much of the country was still raw. Guns put meat on the table and defended the family; shooting skill was admired, and hunting for sport held some glamour. And during Hemingway's life America raised two enormous citizen armies, millions more people who came to see guns as everyday tools.

Hemingway's friend and biographer A.E. Hotchner wrote that on his first visit to the Finca Vigía, Ernest's home outside Havana, the author showed him "a yellowed four-by-five picture of Ernest, aged five or six, holding a small rifle. Written on the back in his mother's hand was the notation, 'Ernest was taught

*Walloon Lake, Michigan, summer 1904. Ernest Miller Hemingway at the age of 5, posing with a break-action Markham King air rifle that then sold for about 75¢. Markham Co. advertisements pointed out that "Every live, healthy boy wants a 'King' Air Rifle. It's boy nature to want a gun; to want to get out in the fields and woods, nearest to nature, and enjoy youthful life to its fullest extent. Get your boy a 'King' Air Rifle. It will mean health and boyish happiness—and steady nerves, keener eyesight and well-developed powers of observation." Eyesight aside, Hemingway became a convincing testament to Markham's claim.*

John F. Kennedy Library

birds and big game in Michigan, Arkansas, Maine, New York, Florida, Idaho, Montana and Wyoming; in France and Italy, Greece, Spain and Cuba, and probably elsewhere. He shot pigeons in competition in the US and in Cuba and Europe. He went on two long and celebrated safaris in East Africa, in 1933 and 1953, where he was guided by one of the white hunters who had accompanied Theodore Roosevelt on his 1910 expedition. "White hunter" was a perfectly acceptable term in his day.

Hemingway sprinkled hunting and shooting narratives throughout his work, but most of them appear in his books (*Green Hills of Africa*, *Under Kilimanjaro* and *True at First Light*) and the two famous short stories, "Snows of Kilimanjaro" and "The Short Happy Life of Francis Macomber," set in Africa; in the Nick Adams stories; in his "Letters" to readers of *Esquire* in the 1930s; and in articles that appeared in *Look* and other magazines, even *Vogue*. Somewhat mysteriously, his novel *The Garden of Eden*, which is about a man who loses his wife to a lesbian lover, contains a long and emotional, loss-of-innocence description of hunting an old bull elephant for his ivory. In fact, though, everything Hemingway wrote came

to shoot by Pa when 2½ and when 4 could handle a pistol.'" [1] His grandfather Anson Hemingway gave him a single-shot 20-gauge shotgun on his tenth or twelfth birthday. Ernest was a member of his high school gun club and went to war when he was 18.

Hemingway hunted waterfowl, upland

from the perspective of a hunter. Hunting was the context for his life, or of life itself. What more appropriate setting than one where effort and risk, predation and death are always present? Hemingway distilled energy and struggle from hunting and managed to express the well-being, fears, pride, jealousies, largesse and accomplishments of being human and male, married and in love, egotistical but self-deprecating, publicly successful while privately striving and doubtful.

Hemingway also had a highly developed sense of what should have been, as opposed to what really happened, a theme he returned to often: "My excuse is that I make the truth as I invent it truer than it would be." (This appears in *Under Kilimanjaro* and *True at First Light*, and elsewhere.) To be true in all aspects of his writing, he had to know the truth of all aspects of hunting, especially the guns and the game and the etiquette that saves lives in the field and sanity in camp.

Did he get it right? Did he speak *truly*?

## TALK TO ME!

Our research began in September 2007 and has extended from Sun Valley to Key West and from the Police Firearms Bureau in Nairobi to the John F. Kennedy Library in Boston, which houses the Hemingway archive. It has included all of the Hemingway family autobiographies and many books about Hemingway, scholarly and otherwise; *Look, Life, True, Ken, Esquire, Vogue, Gunsport, Rogue*, the *New Yorker* and other period magazines and newspapers; sporting-goods and

*Michigan, c. 1913. Hemingway in his early teens with what appears to be a crow in one hand and his father's lever-action Winchester shotgun in the other—a Model 1887 for black-powder cartridges, apparently (by the diameter of its barrel and magazine) the 10-gauge version. Hemingway's life reached from the very end of the Wild West to the birth of the Space Program.*     John F. Kennedy Library

auction-house catalogs; gunmakers in the US and abroad; corporate and cultural histories; countless letters that Ernest wrote; and telephone, e-mail and personal conversations with surviving Hemingway friends and family members. Hemingway bought many guns from Abercrombie & Fitch, the New York retailer that closed in 1977, and the owner of those records, Griffin & Howe, made them available to us.

Some things became very clear. For all his passion as a hunter and shooter, not to say his considerable income, Hemingway was never a collector or aficionado of fine guns simply as works of art. He nearly always spent his money on function, not purely esthetic touches such as extra engraving or fancy wood. As he wrote to his friend Milford Baker early on, discussing a new rifle, "I don't care about the job being too ultra, would prefer fit and sturdiness and absolute dependability of action to finish." Forty years later, Hotchner recalled that Hemingway "liked the simple, 'pure' (to use his word) guns he had used all his life. If there was anything he taught me, it was that—respect for good, simple, well-fitted equipment, and a simple, 'primitive' attitude toward hunting itself."[1] Some of his guns were far from simple, but they were never merely ornate.

He also valued the familiarity he'd built up with certain guns over time. Favorites like his Springfield and the Model 12, though well cared for, became battered and bruised and bare of finish from decades of use.

With the exception of one unusual shotgun from France, Hemingway chose guns and calibers from America, England, Italy, Belgium, Austria, Spain and Germany. Some of these were already traditional in his time; some were of cutting-edge design but have become classics in the decades since. Hemingway had an eye for quality and utility, which all of the guns in this book have in common, and he knew how to buy secondhand.

Some things will never be entirely clear. Hemingway was a wealthy, generous and often impulsive man whose closest friends and relatives loved to shoot almost as much as he did. He bought, borrowed, loaned out and gave away guns throughout his life, and a comprehensive listing of them is impossible. Typically, we began with a line that mentioned a certain rifle or shotgun or handgun. We read everything that might be related, including what letters we could get our hands on. We combed the archive at the JFK Library for photographs of the gun. G&H's Bob Beach searched the Abercrombie & Fitch ledgers to see if it had passed through those doors. We begged the maker for factory records. Sometimes, rarely, a Hemingway friend or relative said, "Oh, yes, I remember that one . . . ." Surprises and complications always arose: One Mannlicher became two and then three, but then the photographic, written or anecdotal evidence didn't agree. Could there have been four? Following these threads took us deep into the life of a unique man and often into strong historical currents.

Weapons are some of our most culturally and emotionally potent artifacts. The choice of guns can be as personal as the car one drives or the mate one marries: another expression of wealth, status, education, experience, skill and personal style. Hemingway's guns, as well as how he acquired them and

*Idaho, fall 1941. The family that shoots together (from left): Gregory, Jack, Papa, Martha and Patrick setting out on a late-October day. "Gigi" might have been the most gifted shot of them all; here he carries a smallbore single-shot gun. Jack, contemplating his father's Browning Superposed, became known as a fly fisherman, but bird hunting stayed with him all his life. Hemingway holds his beloved Model 12 Winchester pumpgun. A year earlier, Marty had been given a 20-gauge Winchester Model 21 side-by-side engraved with her initials, which may be under her arm here. "Mouse," cradling perhaps the other family Model 21, made hunting his life; from 1951 until 1975 he was a white hunter, a forestry officer and an instructor of game wardens and professional hunters in East Africa.* Lloyd Arnold/John F. Kennedy Library

what he did with them, tell us about Hemingway as a man. Every hunter, shooter or collector has examined a well-worn gun of some sort and thought: *Who used this thing? Where has it been? What great adventures was it part of?* *Talk to me!* To some extent, we've been able to make Papa's guns talk.

— *Silvio Calabi*
*Steve Helsley*
*Roger Sanger*
*July 2010*

— 9 —

# A Firearms Vocabulary

The word "gun" loosely refers to any firearm, but strictly speaking it means a shotgun, not a rifle. The term is sometimes used interchangeably in this book, but the context should clarify whether the reference is to a shotgun or a rifle. As a hunter of gamebirds as well as animals, Ernest Hemingway had both.

A rifle (or a handgun) fires a single projectile—a bullet. The word comes from "rifling," the half-dozen or so grooves cut along the bore, the inside of the barrel, in long spirals. The bullet is a tight fit in the bore; the rifling makes it spin in flight, for stability and accuracy. A hunting rifle should put its bullets into a one-inch circle at a hundred yards, but in the field the shooter's skill and steadiness contribute more to accuracy than the rifle's mechanical consistency. The practical maximum range for a hunting rifle is about 400 yards, but most hunters are well advised to stay within half that distance—depending on visibility, weather, the animal and the rifle, and again personal experience and ability.

The diameter of the bullet/bore is the caliber, expressed in millimeters for Continental rifles or modern military weapons (8mm, say, or 5.56mm) and in decimal fractions of an inch (.308, for example, or .303) for American and British rifles. There may be many proprietary versions of a given caliber, such as .300 Weatherby, .300 Winchester Magnum, .300 H&H Magnum, .300 Dakota and so on, all different in certain dimensions and performance and none interchangeable.

A shotgun is a "smoothbore"—no rifling in the barrel—meant to shoot clusters of pellets, usually lead, that spread out in flight. This makes it possible to hit a bird on the wing out to about 50 or 60 yards. Shotguns are inherently short-range weapons; while a high-velocity rifle bullet may carry for several miles (if the barrel's muzzle is elevated enough), even the largest birdshot pellets fall to earth within 300 or 400 yards. At very close range the ounce or so of pellets in a typical shot cartridge doesn't have time to spread out much, so inside 20 feet a shotgun blast is highly lethal and destructive, no matter whether the gun was loaded with fine birdshot or large buckshot. Beyond that distance the spread of the pellets can be controlled somewhat by "choking" the barrel at the muzzle—constricting its bore slightly. A full-choke barrel delivers a tighter cloud of pellets downrange than an open barrel—putting most of the shot inside a two-foot circle, approximately, at 40 yards.

Shotguns are measured in gauge. While for a rifle a higher caliber means a bigger bore diameter, on a shotgun a higher gauge number is a smaller bore. Gauge is the number of balls that could be made from one pound of lead that each just fit the inside diameter of the barrel. This comes from early cannon designation. A 12-pounder cannon (a cannon is a gun—no rifling) fires a 12-pound ball; a 12-gauge gun is a 1/12-pounder. Twelve is still the most popular shotgun gauge. A 1/12-pound lead ball is 0.729 inches in diameter. Hence 12 gauge measures .729 caliber— nearly three-quarters of an inch, far larger than any sporting-rifle bore because of the need to accommodate the several hundred pellets in a typical shotgun cartridge.

A cartridge, also known as a round, is a single unit of ammunition. For a rifle or handgun, this is a bullet wedged into the mouth of a metal case, or shell, that holds the gunpowder and has, in its base, a primer. A shotgun cartridge is much the same, but its shot charge is contained in a plastic (sometimes waxed cardboard) sleeve with a metallic base for the powder and primer. Both kinds of cartridges can usually be reloaded and reused.

A cartridge is a precise fit in the chamber, the first section of the gun barrel. Inside the action, the firing pin, driven by a spring-loaded hammer, strikes the primer, which ignites the powder that propels the bullet or shot charge downrange. After a cartridge has been fired, the empty shell must be removed (extracted or ejected) before the chamber can be reloaded. There are at least five basic mechanisms that accomplish this clearing-reloading process in modern rifles and shotguns: bolt action; pump, or slide, action; break action, with single or double barrels arranged side-by-side or over/under; semi-automatic; and lever action. Each has its pros and cons as well as its fans and detractors.

By law and by sporting tradition and ethics, a rifle, shotgun or handgun for hunting or target shooting fires one round at a time; the trigger has to be pulled once per shot. A firearm that shoots as long as its trigger is held back is an automatic weapon—a machine gun, forbidden to unauthorized civilians in America since the National Firearms Act of 1934.

*Idaho, probably 1940 or '41. Hemingway with, from right, "Colonel" Taylor Williams, the Sun Valley Resort's chief hunting and fishing guide; movie-maker Howard Hawks; and Gary and Rocky (wife Veronica) Cooper. At this point the Model 12 is only a dozen years old, but it already appears to have seen most of an ordinary lifetime's use.* John F. Kennedy Library

# THE MODEL 12 PUMPGUNS

*I bought a 12 gage winchester which will come in handy around Key West.*
—to Waldo Peirce, 9 August 1928, while Hemingway was in Big Horn, Montana

Exactly why a 12-gauge Winchester would be especially handy around Key West never becomes clear, but Hemingway made very good use of this gun for many years to come, in Cuba, Idaho and even East Africa:

*Ngui had been loading the Winchester 12-gauge pump with SSG which is buckshot in English. We had never shot anything with SSG and I did not want any jams so I tripped the ejector and filled it with No. 8 birdshot cartridges fresh out of the box and filled my pockets with the rest of the cartridges. At close range a charge of fine shot from a full-choked shotgun is as solid as a ball and I remembered seeing the effect on a human body with the small hole blue-black around the edge on the back of the leather jacket and all the load inside the chest.* [1]

Here, on his second African safari, in 1953-'54, Hemingway is preparing to follow a wounded leopard into thick brush. In anticipation of a close-quarters encounter, he has exchanged his rifle for a shotgun: his Model 12 Slide Action Hammerless Repeating Shotgun, manufactured in New Haven, Connecticut, by the Winchester Repeating Arms Company. Unlike traditional double-barreled guns from Britain or Europe, which were largely handmade for the carriage trade and could fire only two rounds before reloading, multi-shot pumpguns are a uniquely American design, one that put mass-produced firepower into everyone's hands. They have a single barrel with another tube, usually shorter, underneath: the magazine, where the ammu-

*Papa's original 12-gauge Winchester Model 12, Serial No. 525488, made in 1928, resembled this gun, with a 30-inch Full-choke barrel, a "corncob" forend and a solid rib. Fresh shells were loaded into the magazine tube, beneath the barrel, through the port on the floor of the action, just ahead of the trigger guard.*

Ron D. White

nition is stored. The gun's foregrip is attached to an actuating bar that slides back and forth. After a shot is fired, pulling the grip back a few inches ejects the spent shell through a port on the side of the action, lets a fresh round feed backward out of the magazine tube, and re-cocks the gun; pushing the grip ahead again brings the new cartridge up and into the firing chamber and locks the action. Now the gun is ready to shoot once more. A skilled hand can work this pull-push pumping action in an eyeblink.

Winchester's Model 1912 shotgun made its debut in that year; the name was shortened to Model 12 in 1919. It was offered first as a 20-gauge and then, two years later, in 16 and 12 gauge as well. The civilian version held up to six rounds in the magazine plus one in the chamber.

Before the First World War, much of the United States was a still-raw land of vast wild-bird populations, market hunting and no bag limits, and many people relied on shotguns for self-defense as well as food, not mere sport. The more cartridges a gun could fire between reloadings, the better. With its exposed-hammer Model 1897, Winchester—already renowned for its rifles that had helped "win the West"—had staked a claim to the pump-action shotgun market too. Just 15 years later the company achieved an astonishing leap forward with the beautifully streamlined and simplified Model 12, lighter and quicker-handling than the '97. Thanks to its speed, reliability and durability, not to say a certain industrial elegance, it became known as the Perfect Repeater. It is arguably still the best pumpgun ever made, and it is no accident that the Model 61, Winchester's successful pump-action .22 rifle, resembled it so closely. (It was probably no coincidence either that Hemingway owned an M61 also.)

Sportsmen bought the M12 mostly to shoot gamebirds such as pheasants, ducks and geese and to compete in clay-target games such as skeet and trap. Unlike many other off-the-rack repeaters, the sleek Model 12 had the balance and liveliness necessary for this kind of dynamic gunning. The M12 could even be "slam-fired," simply pumped as fast as possible while the trigger was held back. This

*The Model 12 had a feature especially useful to the traveling shooter: With no tools and in just seconds, the barrel, magazine and forend of the "Perfect Repeater" could be detached from the receiver for easier packing into case or duffel.*     Ron D. White

feature didn't much benefit hunters, but it helped make the Model 12 a favorite also with police officers and soldiers who relied on shotguns in buildings, trenches, tunnels and other close quarters. (In the 1970s slam-firing was deemed a safety hazard, or at least a legal liability, and thereafter all pumpguns were fitted with interruptors so the trigger has to be pulled separately for each shot.)

The Model 12 had one more feature, one especially useful to the traveling shooter: With no tools and in just seconds, the barrel, magazine and forend could be detached from the receiver for easier packing into case or duffel. Winchester even made accommodation for any possible wear on the mating parts by providing a range of adjustment in the takedown mechanism.

From 1912 to 1963, when Winchester discontinued regular production of it, and then again in the 1970s, close to two million M12s were produced—in 14 styles and 12, 16, 20 and 28 gauge (in a variety of

*Cuba, 1943-'44, probably at the Club des Cazadores del Cerro, where the Hemingways shot boxed birds. Third son Gregory, "Gigi," won a gold medal there in 1941, at the age of 9, by out-shooting 24 men on live pigeons—with a .410. Papa was button-burstingly proud. Hemingway holds his Model 12; Gigi may be carrying his stepmother Marty's 20-gauge Model 21.*

John F. Kennedy Library

chamber lengths) and with plain, stippled or ribbed barrels from 25 to 32 inches long and bored in all possible chokes. There were even, briefly, barrels made of stainless steel. If the variety of factory-issue models didn't suit, the Winchester Custom Shop stood ready to make anything a client wanted, for a price. Hemingway's Model 12 was a plain 12-gauge, dated by its serial number to 1928, with a solid rib and what became known as the "corncob" forend. Patrick recalled that years later, long after his father had become world-famous and well-heeled, he liked to shoot his Model 12 even in situations where, because it was so utilitarian, it offended other people. By virtue of more than three decades in his hands and hundreds of thousands of rounds fired through it, this otherwise ordinary but excellent shotgun became a Hemingway icon.

In Hemingway's time almost every serious American hunter owned a Model 12, had owned one or wanted one—a situation that Winchester aided and abetted by sending professional shooters around the country to demonstrate the gun's capabilities. It was not inexpensive; in 1914 a field-grade 12-gauge cost $32 (the equivalent of $685 in 2010), a working man's wages for a week or more. By 1963, the final year of regular production, the same gun cost $110—only slightly more, adjusted for inflation. That year an internal audit revealed that Winchester was losing money on several of its most popular products and that machining the receiver of the M12 was especially time-consuming and expensive.

Instead of raising prices, the company's new management chose to cut corners with its legendary quality instead. In 1964 the standard Model 12 was replaced by a more cheaply built gun called the Model 1200. A few M12s were made as late as 1980 but, as historian Ned Schwing wrote, "The finesse of the old craftsmanship was gone. They simply cast the parts, assembled and blued them, and out the door they went." Today a pre-1964 serial number on any Winchester adds to its value, and original Model 12s are prized, although not expensive. Even the plain-jane versions long ago transcended their utilitarian roots.

There is little mention of his Model 12 in *Green Hills of Africa*, the "nonfiction novel" of his first safari, in 1933-'34, but a year earlier Hemingway had written to his pal Mike Strater, "I am taking [to Africa] 30.06—10.75 Mauser—12 ga shotgun (pump) and 6.5 Mannlicher—also my Colt 22 cal Woodsman" [2] and on page 70 in the book he writes, "I fed shells into the magazine of the old Winchester pump," so it is safe to say that he had this gun with him on his first as well as the second safari, 20 years later. Its serial number, 525488, determined from Abercrombie & Fitch records, dates it to 1928. It was not, in fact, "old" yet in 1933, but its owner was already then noted for his fiction.

Hemingway brought his M12 to East Africa as naturally as he would have packed a toothbrush, and "Pop" (his white hunter on both safaris, Philip Percival), although English, surely recognized it instantly. Its primary purpose was to shoot waterfowl, francolin

*Cuba, probably 1940-'42. Shooting the Model 12 at the Club des Cazadores; note the empty shell in the air.*                                   John F. Kennedy Library

and guinea hens for the table and as a diversion from big game, but because of its short-range lethality and lively handling the gun was also a superb self-defense weapon. From *Under Kilimanjaro* again:

*Ngui came to say . . . would I put the Sten gun together. The Sten gun was the old Winchester Model 12 pump gun and the threading of the aged barrel and receiver together was a mystery. They all believed it was an automatic weapon since it could be fired faster than any automatic shotgun . . . and they would never assemble it for fear of cross threading. It takes twenty thousand cartridges to break in a pump gun so that it handles quicker than your eye can follow and this gun had shot around two hundred thousand cartridges. . . . it*

*was regarded as a straight witchcraft gun and it was never used unless we needed meat badly or for backing up or for going in as for the leopard. It was a goose, guinea, and leopard gun and a back-up gun on lion.* (391)

High-quality pumpguns are like any well-made machine. Over time, given maintenance and lubrication and thousands of cycles, the moving parts mesh together and rough spots disappear. (His father, Patrick recalled, was a believer in Marvel Mystery Oil and used it liberally on this gun: "You could work the slide with one finger." [3]) In the right hands, a well-broken-in Model 12 could literally be made to shoot faster than a Sten, the British police and military submachine gun of the time, despite the Sten's cyclic rate of around 500 rounds per minute. By the 1950s, Kenyan law demanded that repeating shotguns be fitted with plugs to reduce their magazine capacity (and their capacity for slaughter) to two rounds. However, such a law is difficult to enforce in the field, and plugs are easy to remove. The Winchester, with its seven-round capacity, could be "shot dry" much quicker than the 32-round Sten, and Hemingway's 12-gauge shotgun loads were far more powerful than the Sten's 9mm pistol ammunition.

*U*nder *Kilimanjaro* and its shortened edition, *True at First Light*, are about the safari that Ernest and Mary Hemingway took from September 1953 through January 1954. Toward the end of the trip and hunting alone with his .30-06 rifle, Hemingway knocked a stock-killing leopard off a branch some 60 feet up in a tree. As he tells the story, the shot looks and feels good and the cat crashes to earth. But when he and the trackers go to the spot, there is no dead leopard. Instead they find a blood trail that leads into a thicket so dense a man can only crawl in after it. This is when Hemingway exchanges his rifle for the shotgun and replaces the untried buckshot cartridges with shells that had proven they wouldn't jam in the gun. And then:

*It was not very easy to go to the leopard. Ngui had the Springfield .30-06 and he had the good eyes. Pop's gun bearer had the .577 which would knock him, the gunbearer, on his ass if he shot it and he had as good eyes as Ngui. I had the old, well-loved, once burnt up, three times restocked,* *worn smooth old Winchester Model 12 pump gun that was faster than a snake and was, from thirty-five years of us being together, almost as close a friend and companion with secrets shared and triumphs and disasters not revealed as the other friend a man has all his life.* [1]

Today, no Professional Hunter will let a client hunt alone, much less deal with a wounded leopard. "Pop" could allow his client so much freedom in part because Denis Zaphiro, a Kenya Game Ranger, or warden, was with the Hemingways while he, Percival, was away. As well, the Game Department had appointed Hemingway an honorary warden for the Kajiado District of southern Kenya—something Hemingway was proud of and took seriously. Hence his pursuit of this *shamba*-raiding cat.

(Honorary wardens were intended to augment Kenya's woefully understaffed game-ranger corps. The title conferred real authority and the power to shoot "on control"—to kill problem animals, on license or not. It was highly unusual to appoint a visiting safari client to the position, but Hemingway was, well, Hemingway; he was in the bush for months, instead of weeks; and both Percival and Zaphiro must have supported this. In addition, EAPHA, the East African Professional Hunters Association, voted at its 23 December '53 meeting to make Hemingway an associate member.)

In this instance the author truly was on his own, acting as a warden—Zaphiro was away on Game Department business and Percival had gone home to his farm near Macha-

*Idaho, fall of 1947 or '48. Hemingway enjoyed teaching women to shoot—and what man wouldn't like to coach actress Jane Russell? She was one of the celebrities drawn to Sun Valley in part by its natural beauty and partly by the presence of Papa himself.*                    John F. Kennedy Library

kos—with no professional to take over this nasty situation. Nowhere in the world does an ethical hunter walk away from an injured animal. Its suffering should be ended; and a wounded dangerous animal is a threat to anyone in the vicinity—unsuspecting locals, for example. Hemingway knew he had to cinch up his manhood and proceed with the

job. Ten years earlier, he had written:

*In the ethics of shooting dangerous game is the premise that the trouble you shoot yourself into you must be prepared to shoot yourself out of.* [4]

In his Model 12, Hemingway chose a potent weapon that was not only reliable and could be operated in a blur of movement, but evidently also was as familiar to him as a prime part of his male anatomy—even if he'd owned the gun for possibly only 25 years at that point (1928 to 1953), not 35. He crawled after the leopard as well prepared as possible, but the outcome was not to be taken for granted. Like his literary predecessor in East Africa's gamefields, Theodore Roosevelt, Hemingway suffered from poor vision and often wore eyeglasses to shoot—a serious handicap in heat and thick brush. And in addition to being middle-aged and well-rounded, Hemingway also had a bad right knee, courtesy of a mortar round in northern Italy in 1918. To maneuver a long-barreled gun in a thicket, on one's belly or knees and while peering through glasses, is difficult even without the gut-clenching threat of sudden attack. If the cat had leaped on him, Hemingway would not necessarily have been saved by Ngui and the gunbearer, either, even though they were carrying rifles. In that kind of rolling, screaming mêlée, odds are that they would have shot Hemingway as readily as the leopard.

The story ends without a charge. The cat was too hurt to get to its feet and, to everyone's great relief, Hemingway eventually killed it without further difficulty.

In December 1931 a fire in "Uncle Gus" Pfeiffer's barn in Piggott, Arkansas (converted to a guest house, where Ernest and Pauline stayed), had destroyed Hemingway's typewriter, some boots and clothing and several of his guns. If this "once burnt-up, three times restocked" Model 12 was one of them, its steel parts survived the fire and Hemingway may have fitted a new buttstock and forend,

a simple repair. This was during the "waste not, want not" years of the Depression, but by 1931 Hemingway was becoming financially secure—*A Farewell to Arms* had just been made into a movie. A new shotgun was surely within reach. Nonetheless, a hunter and shooter of Hemingway's upbringing would not junk a good gun lightly.

Hemingway was then married to his second wife, Pauline Pfeiffer, who came from a wealthy family. Gustavus Pfeiffer, Pauline's uncle, was a successful pharmaceuticals and cosmetics entrepreneur who became close to the Hemingways. He traveled with them and paid for not only the Hemingways' house in Key West, but also their 1933-'34 safari, which he saw as an investment in his nephew-in-law's writing career.

Around 1958, Papa declared that his Model 12 was worn out. His Idaho friend Lloyd Arnold wrote that it was "a weapon you wouldn't give ten dollars for if seen in a hock-shop window—that is, unless you were a lover of Model 12's. It rattled like a corn-sheller in 'loose as a goose action' and light oil spray flew out of it in a cloud when you slammed home the breech. The over-oiling had settled into the grip of the stock which was split where it butted the metal and was so loose it was about to fall off." [5] Hemingway replaced it with another Model 12, a short-barreled 12-gauge with a Flex-Choke on its muzzle that he bought from a hotel bellboy in Sun Valley. (The gun was at the resort so that the famous trapshooter, Rudy Etchen, could test the choke

*Idaho, fall 1960. In the foreground, wringing a mallard's neck, is rancher Bud Purdy; his wife Ruth is in the background. Papa is holding another mallard, which the unidentified hunter seems to be squeezing. Under Papa's arm is his second Model 12, the short-barreled 12-gauge bought from a hotel bellboy. The bulbous device on its muzzle is a Flex-Choke, a gas-operated gadget that automatically tightened the choke with each shot.*                    Lloyd Arnold/John F. Kennedy Library

device. When the testing was done, Etchen had sold the Winchester to the bellboy.) Hemingway shifted easily to the newer gun. Arnold saw Papa in action with it in the fall of 1960, less than a year before his death:

"The sharp click of the action homing one in the chamber spooked a triple of mallard drakes hugging the low near bank of the sluggish water—all nicely in range. Papa exploded into action, as fast as I had ever seen him go. He nailed a double neatly, tried for a triple, the lead bird a wee bit out of range. It was flawless gun-handling . . . ." [5] The serial number of this gun remains unknown, as does its fate after its owner's death on 2 July 1961.

Hemingway's original Model 12, No. 525488, with a 30-inch Full-choke barrel, was one of four guns consigned to Abercrombie & Fitch by Mary, his widow, on 3 July 1963. It was sold a month later. John Nodop, the buyer, was 20 years old then, a college student from Connecticut who sometimes visited Abercrombie's seventh floor—the famous gunroom—after having lunch with his father, who worked in Manhattan. Abercrombie & Fitch, in a 12-story building on the corner of Madison Avenue and 45th Street in Manhattan, was America's most famous "outfitter" from 1910 until its closure in 1977. It catered to sportsmen and women of all kinds, but it was the absolute center of the universe for hunters and shooters. Ernest Hemingway did business with A&F for all of his adult life.

"I couldn't figure out why Abercrombie's had such a beat-up, cheap gun," John Nodop remembered. "The finish was practically gone, but mechanically it was all there, and I wanted it. My father loaned me the money and I went in the next day and the gun was still there, so I bought it.

"The receiver was pitted. The salesman told me it had been used by a duck hunter out on Long Island Sound, in the salt water.

"It had a 30-inch barrel and was one of the tightest-choked guns I've ever encountered. I either missed entirely or blew the bird to pieces. It had a solid rib, which had begun to separate from the barrel near the end of the grip, just enough to get a fingernail into the gap.

"The stock was heavily worn. It had a corncob grip and the grooves were almost worn away, especially on the bottom. And it was black there. I had the gun re-done out in Holland, Michigan, at a place just a block from where I went to school. The finish was down to a gray patina all over. The gunsmith said the pits were too deep to take out, so he just buffed it lightly and re-blued it. Then I bought a bird's-eye-maple stock blank with a rollover comb from Herter's; a friend and I took a lot of wood off it with a band saw. Then it handled beautifully. I replaced the forend as well, also with bird's-eye maple.

"You could cycle the action with one finger—it was flawlessly smooth. The bore was shiny as a mirror. That was my first shotgun.

"I traded it around 1980 at the gunshop on Main Street in Jeffersonville, New York, for a Spanish side-by-side called a Dixon Falcon. Made by Ugartechea. It was about a $90 gun, and I got maybe $40 for the Model 12 as a trade-in.

"I have no idea where it went after that."

John Nodop, now a retired US Air Force chaplain, paid $35 for Papa's Model 12 Winchester in 1963 and, until December 2009, when the authors of this book found and interviewed him, he believed it had been someone's knockabout Long Island duck gun.

# THE BROWNING SUPERPOSED

*So I . . . told Ernest he'd have to have poured it on to win that cracking good Browning over-under double barrel 12 gauge.*

—Lloyd Arnold, *High on the Wild with Hemingway*, page 32

The "cracking good" Browning shotgun that Hemingway proudly showed off to Lloyd Arnold—in room 206 at the Sun Valley Lodge, in the fall of 1939, when Ernest and Martha Gellhorn first visited the resort—was something unusual for that time in the American West. "Over/under" guns are, like side-by-sides, also break-action (hinged in the middle) double-barrel types, but their tubes are mated vertically instead of horizontally. Until about 1930 such guns were largely the products of English and Continental makers and sold at prices only the wealthy could afford. Hemingway's Browning, though manufactured in Europe and not inexpensive, was the first "mass-market" version of an over/under, and it seems that his came from a source close to its origin. Apparently he acquired it in an unusual way and then put it to long and good use. And then it disappeared.

Centuries ago, when firearms had to be loaded by pushing powder, shot and wadding down the barrel from the muzzle—a laborious process—the easiest way to get more than one shot was to have more than one barrel. Early multi-barreled guns often had their tubes stacked one atop the other. As gunmaking became more sophisticated, this design went out of favor until, by the beginning of the 19th Century, most double-gun barrels were set horizontally. (Among other things, this may have reflected the general agreement that virtually every shooter's eyes were also positioned side by side.) The slow prolifera-

*Ernest Hemingway's Browning resembled this gun—a pre-1936 Grade I Superposed with no engraving; a Jostam Hy-Gun recoil pad; and double, possibly "Twin-Single," triggers—with the addition of a low-step rib and the longer, squared-off Target forend.*
James D. Julia Auctioneers

tion of practical breechloaders—guns whose barrels could be loaded, much more conveniently, from the rear—beginning early in the 1800s vindicated the side-by-side layout as, in some respects, side-by guns are simpler to make than over/unders and they need not be opened as far to reload. (The barrels of an over/under have to pivot down farther in order to expose the lower tube.) The evolution of the side-by-side gun peaked in about 1890 and has not budged since. However, markets demand variety, and by 1900 over/under double guns were again being developed.

In London, Boss & Company introduced the first well-known modern over/under in 1909. The firm is still in business, and its made-to-order guns, side-by-sides and over/unders, sell for six-figure sums. In 1913 James Woodward, also in London, began to offer an "under and over" gun made to his design, in even smaller numbers and also at stratospheric prices. (James Purdey & Sons bought the rights to the Woodward in 1948 and continues to offer it.) Other British gunmakers dallied with the vertical-barrel format, but none achieved the fame of the Boss. Meanwhile, a rationale for the two types of double-barreled guns emerged: Competition shotgunners, who call for their targets when they're ready to shoot, prefer the over/under so they can sight more deliberately along the single top barrel; hunters, whose targets often appear unexpectedly and from all angles and at all ranges, shoot instinctively and tend to favor the traditional side-by-side layout because of its slightly better dynamic qualities. Today,

however, the over/under is the overwhelmingly dominant double gun in wingshooting everywhere, and the guns come from high-volume industrial manufacturers, mostly in Italy and Japan.

This happened in part because of a firearms genius named John M. Browning, who designed an over/under that could be mass-produced at reasonable cost. Ernest Hemingway, a bona-fide celebrity by the late 1930s, possibly helped make the over/under "the American double gun" also.

John Moses Browning (1855-1926) was a son and apprentice of gunsmith Jonathan Browning, of Ogden, Utah Territory. When his father died, in 1879, John and several of his brothers—there were 22 siblings in this Mormon family—launched the Browning Gun Factory to build John's first patented design, a breechloading single-shot rifle. It was successful enough to catch the eye of a large competitor back East and, in 1883, the Winchester Repeating Arms Company bought the rights to the Browning rifle and began to manufacture and sell it as the Model 1885, which became the famous Winchester "High Wall." Without the burden of running a factory, Browning could concentrate on design and innovation. There followed many Winchester rifles and guns—a partial list includes the Models 1886, 1887, 1890, 1892, 1894, 1895, 1897 and 1901—that were made in Connecticut but designed by John Browning in Utah. Today, the number of John Browning-designed firearms produced under the

*Idaho, fall 1940. A shirt-sleeves day of duck hunting on Silver Creek with the Browning Super-*
*posed. Here a few years later, Papa and son Jack rolled their canoe, dumping the Browning and*
*the Model 12 Winchester—Hemingway's go-to guns in this era—into 10 feet of water.*

Lloyd Arnold/John F. Kennedy Library

— 25 —

*Hemingway with his Browning open over his arm and Wilson's snipe—"delectable little birds that all went into the tribal pot."*

Lloyd Arnold/John F. Kennedy Library

US market and its range of manually operated firearms, wavered. In 1902 Browning approached the Remington Arms Company, in New York, but its president died on the day of their scheduled meeting. No doubt frustrated, John Browning went instead to Belgium, where he struck a deal with Fabrique Nationale d'Armes de Guerre. Now known as FN, the firm was established in 1889 to build Mauser military rifles for the Belgian government; it had also been producing Browning's first semi-automatic pistol, the Model 1900. The Belgians would now manufacture Browning's innovative Automatic 5 shotgun also. (And it too would find a spot in Ernest Hemingway's hunter's heart.)

At the time, Europe was well ahead of the United States in the design and production of self-loading firearms, both military and sporting. Hiram Maxim, from Maine, found the first buyer for his machine gun in Britain in 1889. Mauser was developing a semi-automatic rifle by 1900 and Mannlicher a semi-auto shotgun; pistols were coming from Borchardt, Bergmann, Schwarzlose, Charola-Anitua, Luger and probably others. Thus FN was likely more open to Browning's new designs.

Browning went on to create many military weapons for FN, including the 1917, 1919 and M2 machine guns and the fabled BAR, the Browning Automatic Rifle. (FN today is still a

Winchester name is said to approach 10 million.

For almost 20 years Browning simply sold his inventions outright to Winchester. But by 1900 he was creating semi-automatic and automatic (self-loading and cocking) firearms, and he wanted a different arrangement: royalties on guns produced to his designs. Winchester, content with its majority share of the

major supplier of tactical as well as sporting weapons.) John Browning did business with Colt too, which manufactured his 1895 machine gun and then the world-famous Model 1911 .45-caliber semi-automatic pistol, carried by American and some Allied troops through both World Wars, Korea and Vietnam.

In his lifetime, Browning was awarded 128 firearms patents. One of the most significant of them happened to be the last one, and it changed the sporting shotgun world.

In 1913, after public outcry in the United States over declining wildlife numbers and the commercial slaughter of game for market, the federal government passed the Weeks-McLean Act, better known as the Federal Migratory Bird Law. Among many other things, this limited shotguns to holding and firing no more than three cartridges for hunting. The Migratory Bird Treaty of 1918 expanded this ban internationally, and eventually some countries limited repeating shot-

*Idaho, September 1940. Hemingway, with his Superposed, and Gary Cooper, probably carrying a Model 21 Winchester, meet for the first time. Hemingway's* For Whom the Bell Tolls, *the film version of which would star Cooper, was published a month later. Cooper's contract with Paramount forbid him to wear eyeglasses in public, which made wingshooting difficult. Hemingway usually took his off for the camera.*

Lloyd Arnold/John F. Kennedy Library

guns to just two cartridges. John Browning feared that governments might go further and restrict the manufacture of repeating shotguns themselves. At the time, a handful of companies in the US still produced side-by-side double guns, but Americans were increasingly turning to single-barrel, multi-shot guns such as the Winchester Model 12 and Browning's own A-5.

Browning was well aware of English and European over/under guns and thought that their similarly narrow sighting planes (due to their vertical barrels) would appeal to American shooters, while their built-in limit of two cartridges would satisfy the law. But Browning knew that to bring the price of such guns down to everyday levels he had to greatly reduce the time and labor to manufacture them. In 1922, the world's foremost firearms designer set out to do just this, and in 1926, at the age of 71, Browning was awarded what would be his final patent, for an over/under shotgun that a working man could afford.

It is still known in Britain and Europe as the Model B25, but from the beginning in America it was called the Superposed—from "superimposed," i.e., one barrel above the other. Like most of Browning's designs, it was innovative, and the 1931 Browning catalog pointed out that it was not just an adaptation of a side-by-side gun, but that it had been designed "from the ground up" as an over/under. It had a boxlock action powered by machine-made coil springs instead of the more complex sidelock style, which typically has handmade V springs. The full-length hinge pin across the bottom of the action was stronger and simpler to make and fit than the dual side lugs on handmade over/unders. The B25 action

locked via a rectangular bolt that slid into a slot in the base of the lower barrel, which kept the breech face of both barrels unobstructed for faster loading. Unique among modern double guns, the wooden forend stayed with the barrels when the gun was taken apart, to simplify the job and to reduce the chances of damage or loss. Like the English Boss, the Browning had selective ejectors, which cleared only the empty shell from whichever barrel had been fired. Unlike the Boss, it cost just two weeks' pay, not two years'.

Also unlike the Boss, at first the Superposed was available only with double triggers—one for each barrel. Browning knew that Americans preferred single triggers, but he died before he could perfect his own design. John's son, Val Allen Browning, in 1939 came up with a reliable single-trigger mechanism that also had a barrel selector built into the safety catch. This gave the gun another distinct advantage in the market.

The Browning family incorporated the Browning Arms Company in Utah in 1927, the year after John M. died. This was a sales and distribution company; manufacturing of Browning-branded guns by FN stayed in Belgium. The first Superposed guns arrived in the US in 1931 as 12-gauges with double triggers and pistol-grip stocks, in plain Grade I. The gun initially listed for $107.50, equivalent to $1,500 in 2010, but the Great Depression allowed, or forced, the company to cut the price to $99.50 in 1934 and then further yet. Higher grades—Pigeon, Diana and Midas, differentiated by wood and engraving—

*Idaho, October 1939. Rancher Tom Gooding, left, holds a Model 12 Winchester too shiny to be Hemingway's. Ernest has his Browning Superposed. Gene Van Guilder, the Sun Valley Resort's public-relations man, died in a hunting accident just days later. Resort photographer Lloyd Arnold, right, was an avid hunter and shooter also.*          Lloyd Arnold/John F. Kennedy Library

were offered from the outset. Some 17,000 Superposed guns had been made by 1940, when the German army seized Belgium. Superposed production resumed in 1947. In 1949, the first 20-gauge Superposeds were offered, and in 1959, the model line grew to include 28-gauge and .410-bore guns. In 1950 the base price was $261, which rose to $375 in 1965 and $465 in 1970. By the mid-1970s, the price had climbed to $1,170 (the equivalent of $4,200 in 2010), which drove Browning to develop less-expensive over/unders—the B27 and ST-100—in Belgium and to arrange for the production of a similar-looking gun in Japan. This was the much-less-costly Citori, which appeared in 1973 and is still in produc-

As the Browning ads would say: "Smooth as Silk—Rugged as the Rockies."

*Spain, 1930. Val Browning, Walter Warren and Ben Gallagher pose as the winners of the Team International Pigeon Championships. Browning and Warren shot Superposed guns, Browning B25s. Gallagher (right) is holding a Super-Britte, a rare and unusual side-opening over/under shotgun, also made in Belgium.* The John M. Browning Museum, Ogden Union Station Collection

Ernest Hemingway sailed to France in December of 1921 with his bride, Hadley Richardson, to be a foreign correspondent for the *Toronto Star*. He was just 22 years old but already a decorated veteran of the First World War; as a teenage volunteer, he had driven an ambulance in northern Italy and been wounded in the legs by mortar shrapnel and at least one machine-gun bullet. From 1922 to '28 his principal residence was Paris, where he became part of Gertrude Stein's "Lost Generation" of young American expatriates living the artistic life—F. Scott Fitzgerald, John Dos Passos, John Steinbeck, Cole Porter, Ezra Pound, E.E. Cummings, Sherwood Anderson, Waldo Peirce, Henry

tion. The Belgian B25 was last cataloged as a regular item in 1976, by which time some 255,000 had been built. Today the trade in secondhand Superposed guns is very strong in the US, the United Kingdom and Europe. The gun is still available new by special order; although no longer moderately priced, it is still only one-tenth the price of a bespoke Boss over/under.

Strater and others.

To a couple of intelligent kids from the Upper Midwest, Paris was sophisticated and alive and wonderfully exotic. It was, as well, an inexpensive place to live on American dollars, and no French government would ever dream of anything like Prohibition.

For the next six years, Hemingway's brief was to roam Europe as a writer, and he took

*The Club des Cazadores, Cuba, c. 1942. Martha Gellhorn Hemingway is holding her 20-gauge Winchester Model 21. Three of the four over/unders, including the ones carried by her husband (center) and their friend Winston Guest (second from right), appear to be Browning Superposeds. Roberto Herrera Sotolongo, Hemingway's sometime secretary, called the club a "bastion of Cuba's intellectual bourgeoisie." According to a former club bird boy, quoted in* Juventud Rebelde *(the Newspaper of Cuban Youth) in 2007, Fidel Castro secretly practiced at the club with Hemingway's "famous over/under" in 1953. After the revolution, the club became a school for machine-gunners and the militia.* John F. Kennedy Library

his responsibilities, as well as their opportunities, seriously. Ernest's first son, John Hadley Nicanor Hemingway (Jack, first nicknamed Bumby), was born in Paris on 10 October 1923. The family crisscrossed the Continent by train and by automobile—to learn about bullfighting in Spain, to ski in the Alps, and to hunt and fish and hike and picnic and socialize wherever possible. In 1926 Ernest and

Hadley's marriage ended, and the following year he married Pauline Pfeiffer, of Piggott, Arkansas, with whom he had two more sons, Patrick in 1928 and Gregory in 1931. Pauline and Ernest eventually made their home in Key West, Florida, but Hemingway traveled widely and often for months at a time. He returned to France again and again, and it may have been there, around 1930 that he became friendly with an American named Ben Gallagher.

Gallagher's father had co-founded a chain of grocery and hardware stores based in Omaha, Nebraska, that sold everything from Butter-Nut coffee to its own line of "Pagoma" shotguns (made by the Crescent Fire Arms Company). Ben reportedly had no interest in joining the family business and apparently spent much of his time on properties he owned in Colorado and Michigan and in the Sologne, a rural part of the Loire Valley in east-central France. He competed on the international live-pigeon-shooting circuit in the 1920s and '30s. Intermittently, in the '30s, he and Hemingway visited each other in Europe and Florida and Cuba and shot pheasants and pigeons together.

But the other shotgun had a special significance for him, and he was bursting to tell me about it for he figured I might know the man from whom he'd won it in a live bird shoot in France. In the sporting circles of the Midwest, wealthy sportsman Ben Gallagher's name was synonymous with top shotgunning. I knew him but slightly through former employers of mine—good shots and hunters themselves. So I knew that Ben G was a great shot and told Ernest he'd have to have poured it on to win that cracking good Browning over-under double barrel 12 gauge—choked for short and medium ranges; a short, very handy piece.

"'You're damn right I did.' He laughed. 'Ben made me go over my head, maybe, and when it was over he said, 'And furthermore, now you can take the goddamn gun and . . . .'" [2]

In light of the correspondence between Gallagher and Hemingway and Hemingway's mentions of Gallagher to Arnold Gingrich (founder of *Esquire*, which published a series of short Hemingway "Letters" on hunting and fishing) and to his friend Tommy Shevlin, Lloyd Arnold's account of Hemingway winning the Browning from Ben Gallagher is credible. Furthermore, since Val Browning, son and colleague of John M. Browning, and Ben Gallagher were friends, it is tempting to think that the noted gun designer in Belgium supplied some of his family's ground-breaking new over/unders to his friend, the prominent American pro shooter in France. And from there it is only a small step to imagine the pro shooter putting one of these guns up as a prize that was then won by the celebrated young American author who was himself a consummate shot.

The gun features in many photographs of Hemingway, especially in Idaho, but its serial number remains a mystery, as does its fate. It is clearly a first-generation Grade I B25, produced between 1931 and 1935, and it may be that Hemingway won it in 1934 or later. Had he owned it by the autumn of 1933, it seems likely that he would have taken it to Africa, but it figures in no safari photos or narratives.

Papa was absent from Sun Valley for 10 years beginning in 1948. When he returned, white-haired and in failing health, in the fall of 1958, his old hunting friend Lloyd Arnold asked him "about the two old favorites I knew so well [the Model 12 and the Browning over/under]. Oh, they had faded away along the line, just like old soldiers do, he'd said." [2]

# TWO BROWNING AUTOMATIC 5S

*I shot one (a Browning) for twelve years and it is the only good automatic shot gun.* —To Gen. Charles Lanham, 2 November 1946, while Hemingway was in Sun Valley

The A-5 was another Hemingway gun that came from the fertile mind of John M. Browning, America's firearms mastermind—the others being Ernest's Colt Woodsman .22 pistol, his Superposed shotgun and, indirectly, his Model 12, which, although drawn up by a Winchester engineer named Thomas Crosley Johnson, was the offspring of the Browning-designed Model 1897 pumpgun. Ernest's father's lever-action Model 1887 was also a Browning design.

If the slide-action Model 12 Winchester was "the Perfect Repeater," one might wonder why the Browning Auto-5, the first commercially successful semi-automatic shotgun, was not considered more perfect yet. After all, the Browning reloaded itself; the shooter had merely to pull the trigger for each shot. On the face of it, a self-loading gun should

beat a manually operated one when it comes to putting firepower on a target. Not so: A high-quality, well-broken-in pumpgun can be operated as fast as the shooter's hands can move, which is fast indeed, at least for a very short time and for an expert such as Hemingway, while an automatic gun is limited to the design speed of its mechanism. Although some full-auto weapons—the German MG42 machine gun, for example, capable of 1,200 rounds per minute—could outpace pumpguns by the Second World War, the old Model 12 (and the Remington Model 17, the original Ithaca Model 37 and others) can still operate faster than nearly all semi-automatics, even much newer ones than the A-5. (The same is true for a revolver, a design that goes back to the 17th Century, versus a semi-auto pistol.)

Today, prototype weapons with electron-

*Revolutionary in its day—an early standard-weight 16-gauge Browning Automatic 5, probably very similar to the one Hemingway used in the 1920s and '30s.*
James D. Julia Auctioneers

ic ignition and a radically different type of bullet and magazine can hit instantaneous rates of more than 16,000 rounds per minute, but at the turn of the 19th Century gun designers were still wrestling with mechanical linkages and friction, as well as pressures generated by the new smokeless gunpowder—parameters that Leonardo Da Vinci would have understood.

John Browning completed the design of the Automatic 5 in 1898 and was granted a patent for it two years later. Fabrique Nationale, Browning's new partner in Belgium, began to build the gun immediately and, incredibly, it remained in production for a century, both in Belgium and, after 1974, in Japan. In addition, Browning's long-recoil mechanism became the basis for a number of similar self-loading shotguns manufactured at various times by Remington and Savage in America and Franchi and Breda in Italy. The Tula Armory in Russia produced a knockoff of the Breda version of the A-5 that was called the MC21. (Dmitri Ustinov, the USSR's Defense Minister in the 1970s and a mechanical engineer by training, was a hunter. Someone presented him with one of the semi-auto Bredas. He was impressed with it and sent it to Tula with instructions to "design" a decent shotgun for Russian hunters.[1]) Reportedly, some three million Auto-5-type guns have been made.

Browning built A-5s in 12, 16, 20 and 28 gauge and in styles and configurations that varied from light guns for upland birds to Magnum waterfowlers, and from short-barreled police "riot" models to military versions with extended magazines. The US Army trained anti-aircraft gunners in the Second World War with cut-down A-5s mounted in pivoting cradles, a device that more or less mimicked the 40mm automatic cannon. The practice targets were clay pigeons; the guns were likely Remington Model 11s, as Fabrique Nationale was then in the clutches of the Third Reich.

The "5" refers to the gun's normal capacity—four rounds in the magazine tube beneath the barrel plus one in the chamber. The energy to operate the A-5 mechanism comes from the recoil impulse of each fired cartridge, which drives the barrel and the bolt backward. This movement ejects the spent shell (pulling it from the chamber and kicking it out through a port in the right side of the action body) and re-cocks the internal hammer. Simultaneously, under spring pressure a new cartridge feeds backward out of the magazine and into the action. The return spring then shoves everything forward again, which reseats the barrel, carries the fresh round into the chamber and locks the bolt on it. Now the gun is ready to fire with a pull of the trigger.

In pre-WWI America, where many shotguns still had external hammers that had to be cocked by hand, this was revolutionary.

On 10 December 1931, Hemingway wrote to his friend Henry ("Mike") Strater:

*Have just been to Piggott* [Arkansas, where his Pfeiffer in-laws lived] *shooting quail for a week—swell shooting—killed 3 straight three times—four straight once—the four in the woods—*

*followed them in out of a cornfield—got a double in thick brush . . . .*

*We must hunt there together some fall. You could hunt a new place every day for two months. Lots of peas and beans in the corn for feed. Two years of drought been hard on birds—on account of that I never shot over the limit—12—one day found 7 big coveys—could have killed plenty. Shot my 16 ga Browning.* [2]

In 1931 Browning Arms offered just two shotguns—the brand-new B25 Superposed and the Auto-5, and only the latter was available in 16 gauge. This, reinforced by his comment that "the Browning . . . is the only good automatic shot gun," makes it clear that Hemingway was referring to an A-5. Any firearm designed by John Browning worked well; and any firearm sold under the Browning Arms name was (and still is) made to a high standard. But the A-5 was mass-produced in Europe, where until about 1972 the American dollar was strong, so for most of its run it was competitively priced in the US. If Hemingway bought his 16-gauge in (to pick a possible date) 1929, the listed retail price of the Grade I gun was $49.75, just a dollar more than a standard-grade Model 12 Winchester.

Well made and functional as it was, however, the A-5 had its idiosyncrasies, beginning with its distinctive appearance: Its flat top fell off abruptly at the rear of the action, hence the nickname "humpback" or "squareback." The movement of the barrel and bolt after firing seemed to extend the recoil into a double impact, and then there was a third *whack!* when the barrel slammed forward again. Be-

sides being uncomfortable, all this motion could upset the gun's swing on a fast-moving target for a follow-up shot. And in the rain, water squirted out of the opening where the barrel slid into the receiver. Once the novelty of the self-loading feature wore off, an experienced hand might realize that the A-5 actually shot slower and was bulkier than the lighter, streamlined, slam-firing Model 12. The only "idiosyncrasy" of a Model 12 was the need to pump the action manually, something Hemingway became extraordinarily good at over the decades he shot his M12.

Before the Second World War, the 16 gauge was regarded much as the 20 and the 28 gauge are today—as a light "gentleman's gun" favored by those who didn't have to shoot for the table and could focus on sportsmanship and the esthetic qualities of their gear. Browning, in fact, capitalized on this with its special "Sweet 16," a lightweight Auto-5 produced from 1936 until 1976. But since he had this gun already in 1931, Hemingway's 16-gauge was a standard-weight A-5. He may have decided that his long-barreled, Full-choke 12-gauge Winchester M12 was a bit too much gun for small upland birds such as quail and turned to the 16-gauge A-5 instead. He wrote that he shot it for 12 years—probably from the mid-1920s into the '30s. In that time he went on his first safari (1933-'34) and had to leave the Browning at home since autoloading shotguns were illegal in East Africa. Perhaps he grew to appreciate the Model 12 again in Kenya. In any event, thanks to his new (in 1930) Griffin & Howe .30-06, he was now

*Idaho, probably the fall of 1946. "Slim" Hawks, born Mary Raye Gross in Salinas, California, in 1917, was intelligent and athletic, a model and much-married socialite who divided her time between New York, Los Angeles and Europe. In the 1940s she was the wife of film director Howard Hawks and they were part of the Hollywood contingent that traveled to Sun Valley to play in the outdoors with Hemingway. After the breakup of her marriage to Hawks, she lived for a time with the Hemingways at their home in Cuba. Here she is shouldering a Browning "squareback" with a muzzle device of some sort, probably the 16-gauge with a Cutts Compensator with which she reportedly almost decapitated Hemingway.* John F. Kennedy Library

a confirmed rifleman; as well, on his return from Africa he bought *Pilar,* his boat, and got heavily involved in big-game fishing in the Gulf Stream. Wingshooting may have taken a back seat for a few years.

The serial number, origin and fate of Hemingway's Auto-5 are still not known, and the gun has not surfaced in any photographs.

Years later, Hemingway evidently acquired a second 16-gauge Auto-5 under traumatic circumstances. This one, since it belonged to a woman and could have been of the correct vintage, may well have been a lightweight Sweet 16. It too, however, has disappeared. Hemingway described the incident to his friend Buck Lanham—General Charles T. Lanham, commander of the US 22nd Infantry in France, to whom Papa had attached himself as a war correspondent for *Collier's*—in a letter from Sun Valley on 2 November 1946:

*Had really close piece of business day before yest. As you know women should never be entrusted with automatic weapons and Mrs. Howard (Slim) Hawks proved this again when we were unloading guns to get into the car and she let her 16 gauge Browning off so close to my head that it (literally) singed the hair at base of skull. I was kneeling down fixing boots. She was adequately horrified and I played it very lightly but explained that the weapon was obviously unsafe (not her fault: shit) and so now have come into possession of the weapon which is a very fine one and which you can shoot at Gardiners [Gardiners Island, NY]. Told her would trade it in on an over and under which will be safe for her. But think after that singeing business will bloody well keep the weapon which is a beautifully made and fine functioning job with two barrels and a cutts compensator with four different tubes. I shot one (a Browning) for twelve years and it is the only good automatic shot gun. So what are a few burned hairs off the back of the top of the neck for a piece of loot like that.[2]*

# THE WINCHESTER MODEL 21 SHOTGUNS

*Ernest found Martha's Model 21, 20-gauge Winchester shotgun, and one evening urged me to try shooting it.* —Mary Hemingway, *How It Was*, page 184

For her 32nd birthday, 8 November 1940, Ernest Hemingway had promised Martha Gellhorn, who became his third wife two weeks later, a shotgun. They were already in their second autumn in Sun Valley, and Hemingway was well into the next stage of his uniquely eventful life. In the long run, Idaho had a greater impact on him than Gellhorn did.

A year earlier, in mid-September 1939, Ernest had packed up his black Buick convertible and left Olive and Larry Nordquist's L-Bar-T, in the Clark's Fork Valley of Wyoming. Like Key West in winter, the dude ranch had been his summer and fall refuge through the 1930s, the place where he could write in the mornings and then play—ride, fish, hunt—with his family in the afternoons. ("Play," however, that infused his writing.) But, along with his marriage to Pauline Pfeiffer, that period was over now and he needed a new sanctuary.

Picking up Martha in Billings, Montana, he drove west into Idaho and checked into room 206 in the Sun Valley Lodge. He went not to fish or hunt but to finish *For Whom The Bell Tolls*.

*Winchester Model 21 No. 14267. This was Martha Gellhorn's 32nd-birthday present, bought with money earned from* For Whom The Bells Tolls. *The gun wears its Full-choke, 28-inch long-range barrels; the second pair of barrels, open-choked for shooting at more moderate ranges, have disappeared. Length of pull (from the trigger to the mid-point of the recoil pad) is just 12¾ inches. Like its stablemate, No. 15593, it shows the marks of heavy use but is in excellent working order—typical for favorite Hemingway guns.*

Brad Stanley/John Cymbal: Driven

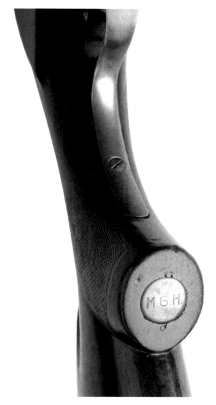

*The grip cap of Model 21 No. 14267 bears Martha Gellhorn Hemingway's initials. (Mary Welsh, wife no. 4, had no middle name and thus no middle initial, "G" or otherwise.)*
Brad Stanley/John Cymbal: Driven

Sun Valley, the brainchild of the Union Pacific Railroad's Averell Harriman, had opened in 1936 as the first ski resort in America. Harriman knew Sun Valley had to be an all-season destination in order to succeed, and he hired fishing and hunting guides, equestrian trainers and even ice-skating coaches in addition to ski instructors. To help spread the word,

Harriman's publicity department invited the influential, famous and connected to Sun Valley, often on the resort's dime. Hemingway, at the age of 40, was all three.

Hemingway's first visit turned into a stay of many weeks and changed his life. Westerners generally did not treat him as a celebrity but judged him on more down-to-earth criteria—could he ride, shoot, drink, treat a lady with respect, tell a good story?—which pleased him. In addition, despite the glamour that would increasingly attach to it, Sun Valley was sheep country, complete with Basque shepherds, which reminded Ernest of the Sierra de Guadarrama, north of Madrid, which he had come to love while covering Spain's Civil War in 1937 and '38. And there was world-class hunting and fishing. Hemingway returned to Sun Valley every fall as often as he could, and after the Cuban revolution he bought a home in nearby Ketchum and ran out the balance of his life in Idaho.

Often rising at dawn to write until late morning, Hemingway might then pack a lunch and go out with the locals who became his close friends. Shooting ducks along Silver Creek, the Big Wood River and in the Hagerman Valley, walking the fields and creek bottoms in the Magic Valley for pheasants and quail, hiking after chukar and Huns in the Picabo Hills, waiting for flights of doves near Timmerman Hill, pounding the sagebrush in Blaine County for grouse, stalking the valley sloughs for snipe—all provided Papa with bird hunting he called the best in the world. In the Sawtooth Mountains there were mule deer and elk, and Hemingway's story "The Shot" is about an antelope hunt in the Pahsimeroi Valley, north of Ketchum.

Naturally, Hemingway never was just one of the gang; he formed and led the gang—"the tribe," as his friends called themselves: Taylor Williams; Lloyd Arnold and his wife Tillie; Clayton Stewart; Pete Hill; Forrest MacMullen; Don Anderson; Win Gray; Bud and Ruth Purdy; Charles Larkin; Tom Gooding; John Powell; Chuck Atkinson; Dr. George Saviers; Clara Spiegel. They were ranchers and professionals and resort staff, locals and transplants, young and middle-aged. Papa's Hollywood friends—among them Gary and Rocky Cooper, Clarke Gable, Ingrid Bergman, Howard and Slim Hawks—came to Sun Valley to hobnob with him too. There was tennis and riding and fishing and famous parties at Trail Creek Cabin, but guns, shooting and hunting often dominated.

Jump-shooting ducks from a canoe was popular. Hemingway took his turn paddling while another hunter shot from the bow, "the throne"; for safety, the paddler in the stern never shot. This was a lesson hard learned. In November 1939, Gene Van Guilder, the young resort publicist who'd lured Hemingway to Sun Valley, was killed while duck shooting from the bow. Lloyd Arnold was in the stern and another man in the middle. Something went wrong. The canoe rolled violently, the middle gun discharged and Van Guilder was shot in the back. Although Hemingway had known him for only six weeks, Van Guilder's widow asked him to speak at the interment.

Twenty-two years later Papa, also victim of a shotgun, was buried two graves away and the famous eulogy he'd written for Van Guilder was said for him as well: "Best of all he loved the fall . . . ."

Jackrabbits were so plentiful that Idaho paid a bounty of 10¢ per animal. They multiplied wildly and sometimes thousands overran a farm and its crops. Hemingway organized rabbit drives, with himself as the "General" of a small army of guns and beaters, with lunch at the farmhouse and hundreds of rabbits taken. Hemingway often supplied the ammunition and gave the bag to the farmer for the bounty. Such random acts of kindness became a Hemingway tradition in Idaho.

Hemingway enjoyed having women take part in his favorite pastimes, no matter what they initially thought of bullfighting or guns or gamefish. According to Ruth Purdy, Hemingway's position was, "When we go hunting, you're going to go hunting," and he took great pleasure in introducing newcomers to shooting. One of these was his fiancée Martha. She admitted to friends that she would prefer to go riding instead, but she bowed to Ernest's wishes and set about learning to handle a shotgun. At first it was a balky pump-action .410—despite its negligible recoil, a notoriously difficult gun to shoot well because of its small shot pattern. Taylor Williams, the resort's chief guide, saw the problem and substituted a double-barreled 20-gauge from his supply of loaner guest guns. Martha's performance immediately improved and Ernest promised that as soon as he came into some money he'd buy her one just like it—a Winchester Model 21.

With the publication of *For Whom The Bell Tolls*, in October 1940, the money began to roll in. Hemingway already had at least one Winchester, the Model 12 pump shotgun he'd acquired more than a decade earlier, and his father Clarence had had a Winchester lever-action shotgun. To a nation for whom the settling of the Wild West was still just a generation or two in the past, the Winchester name was even more familiar and American than Ford or Coca-Cola.

*Idaho, October 1939. Martha Gellhorn with her first birds, probably taken with a 20-gauge Model 21 belonging to the Sun Valley Resort. Her experience with it prompted Ernest to buy her one of her own.*

Lloyd Arnold/John F. Kennedy Library

Unlike Ferdinand Mannlicher, John Browning or William Middleditch Scott, Oliver Fisher Winchester was an unlikely gunmaker. Born on a farm in Massachusetts in 1810, he was apprenticed to a carpenter when he was 14 and became a master builder. Later he opened a retail store, which led to a fortune in men's shirts. In 1855 he invested in the Volcanic Arms Company, in Connecticut (founded by Horace Smith and Daniel Wesson, who went on to handgun fame), which with him as president became the New Haven Arms Company in 1857.

Other American firearms pioneers such as Eli Whitney and Eliphalet Remington were skilled machinists; Oliver Winchester's strengths were promotion, fiscal management and the ability to select talented employees and good products. When the American Civil War erupted, in 1861, Winchester's company was making a lever-action, 16-shot repeating rifle called the .44 Henry. At first the Union's Chief of Ordnance refused to buy it—too fragile, he decided, and it required specialized ammunition. That view was not shared by soldiers, who bought Winchester's rifle and ammunition for themselves. By 1863, the Union and several European governments were also buying, and the company emerged from the war a success. In 1866 Winchester sold the shirt business and re-named New Haven Arms the Winchester Repeating Arms Company. Thereafter all rifles and shotguns, beginning with the Model 1866 and eventually including many designed by John Browning, carried his name. New models and foreign contracts, with particularly large sales to China and Turkey, followed in the 1870s.

When Winchester died, in 1880, his lever-action rifles were—along with Colt's six-shooter—embedded in the world's consciousness as American icons, the "guns of the Wild West," and the business was valued at $3 million.

The company passed to Oliver's son, William Wirt Winchester, who died within three months of his father. William's wife Sarah inherited half of the company and an income of $1,000 a day. After losing not only her husband and father-in-law but then also her daughter, Sarah came to believe the family was cursed because of all the deaths caused by Winchester rifles. A medium advised her to build a house for herself and the spirits—and that if construction ever stopped, she would die. In 1884, in what is now San Jose, California, she started adding rooms to a farmhouse. Construction continued around the clock, seven days a week, 365 days a year for the next 38 years. Upon Sarah's death, in 1922, the house had 160 rooms. Her niece auctioned off the house and employed movers to empty it—eight truckloads a day for six and a half weeks. It is now a National Historic Monument known as the Winchester Mystery House.

After the turn of the 19th Century, Winchester dominated the repeating-shotgun market with its famous Models 1897 and 1912 pumpguns. What Winchester lacked, however, was a double-barreled gun.

By the late 1870s, many of America's leading gunmakers—Colt and Remington, as well as smaller firms such as Parker Bros., L.C. Smith, Fox and Lefever—were building European-style side-by-side shotguns. Winchester was notably absent from this market. In 1878 or '79, the company treasurer, William W. Converse, traveled to England and bought a number of inexpensive Birmingham-built double guns. These sold quickly, although, by most accounts, they were never marked "Winchester." Given this initial success, in 1880 the company decided to import shotguns from Birmingham that would carry the Winchester name. Ultimately, about 10,000 guns—made by W. & C. Scott & Son, among others—were brought into America.

Legend has it that in 1883 P.G. Sanford, the manager of Winchester's New York store and office, complained that it was unseemly for a prominent American arms and ammunition manufacturer to sell imported shotguns. The executive team apparently agreed and, on 12 May 1884, sold the remaining stock of English "Winchesters" to the New York firm of John P. Moore's Sons.

Unseemliness aside, there are two other, more hard-nosed rationales for this decision. The first is that Colt allegedly agreed not to enter the ammunition business if Winchester would stop importing shotguns. (As the Sherman Anti-Trust Act would not be passed until 1890, such collusion was still kosher.) The second explanation seems more likely: Presi-

then the legendary pump-action models—at home, and a double-barreled Winchester gun did not emerge for another 40 years.

To many shooters, particularly in America, the Model 21 was worth the wait. Its design was the sum of contributions by at least five Winchester designers—T.C. Johnson, Edwin Pugsley, George Lewis, Louis Stiennon and Frank F. Burton—over more than a decade, and Winchester would boast that the gun's model name came from the "21 special features incorporated in the design."

American and British makers have never quite agreed on the best configuration for a

*The second Winchester Model 21, also a plain-grade 20-gauge, No. 15593. At some point the stock was shortened to 13½ inches and the leather-covered recoil pad was added. This American-style "beavertail" stock forend—note the wood wrapping up around the barrels—is very different from the minimal British "splinter" forend seen on Ernest's Scott gun.*                    Brad Stanley/John Cymbal: Driven

dent Chester A. Arthur's Tariff Act of 1883 imposed an *ad valorem* duty, a value-added tax, of 35 percent on imported shotguns.

It was time to change direction. Within a few years, Winchester began producing single-barrel repeating shotguns—first John Browning's lever-action Model 1887 and

*The receiver of No. 15593 showing the long action bar and, at the front, a portion of the massive hinge pin on which the barrels pivot. The thumb lever is in the open position.*

Brad Stanley/John Cymbal: Driven

side-by-side double-barreled gun. Best-grade British guns typically have double triggers, slender "splinter"-style stock forends under their barrels, and detachable sidelock actions. American doubles, on the other hand, favor single triggers and larger, wrap-around "beavertail" forends, and are built on less-complex, but arguably stronger, solid-frame boxlock actions.

Nonetheless, the standard boxlock action, patented on behalf of gunmaker Westley Richards in 1875, is a British design, which may explain why Winchester chose to develop its own boxlock mechanism and enough other features sufficiently innovative to earn nine patents for the Model 21.

All firearms are subject to enormous forces at the instant a cartridge is detonated; break-action guns, hinged in the middle, want to open up under these pressures, which makes their locking systems critically important. Not only must they resist this instantaneous shock, they also have to absorb many thousands of rounds before the hinge shows any loosening due to wear. In addition to a sliding underbolt, British and European double guns often have a short extension from the barrels that fits (when the gun is closed) into a slot in the action body and then is pinned by a sliding crossbolt or the like. Winchester's Model 21 had no such extra fastener. Its great strength came from a longer action bar, which reduced the leverage of the detonation, and from unusually stout construction. The gun's barrels were made from Winchester Proof Steel, a patented chrome-molybdenum alloy specially heat-treated to a tensile strength of more than 60 tons per square inch—double the usual. Each barrel began as a solid forged rod and, after machining, the two resultant tubes were fitted to each other across a long, integral vertical dovetail, which was then silver-soldered. While English-style guns have handmade V springs inside, the M21's hammers and ejectors were powered by machine-wound coil springs. The Model 21 also got an improved safety catch and its own reliable selective single-trigger mechanism—one trigger that can be set to fire either barrel first. (Double triggers were an available, extra-cost option.)

When it was officially introduced, in 1931, Winchester described its new top-of-the-line shotgun as "equal in design and quality to any double model anywhere, and of superior design and craftsmanship." In reality, the Model 21 was overbuilt and heavy. The United Kingdom and Europe had, and still have, national proof houses, which test-fire and certify each individual gun made in that country to a certain standard of ammunition. Manufacturers build their guns to those standards and no more, and mark each gun to that effect; the shooter over-loads it to his or her peril. America has never had a proof house, and gunmakers must err on the side of caution to ensure that some unusual, nonstandard ammunition doesn't blow up their products. Using "Violent Proof" loads, with powder charges 50-percent greater than normal, Winchester tested its Model 21 against four US-made competitors. The others failed after firing anywhere from 56 to 305 such cartridges; the M21 was still

*Idaho, fall 1941. Loading up for one of the huge rabbit drives. "General" Hemingway is third from right, pointing his Guns to their posts. The woman under the feathered hat is Anna Roosevelt, daughter of FDR and Eleanor Roosevelt; she and her husband, John Boettiger, were part of Hemingway's circle. (Note the shotgun and shell boxes on the ground.)* John F. Kennedy Library

in good working order after digesting 2,000 of them. The Model 21 remains one of the strongest double guns ever made.

In addition, Winchester produced the Model 21 to unusually exacting specifications; parts were said to be interchangeable from one gun to another, which is not true still today in many double guns, which require final hand-fitting. This was an impressive feat of industrialization in a world where computer-controlled machining was not even imagined yet.

The Model 21 debuted as a 12-gauge for $59.50, equivalent to about $765 in 2010. Given that the Great Depression had just started, this qualified as a master stroke of poor timing. Winchester had gone into receivership in 1930 and was sold to the Western Cartridge Company, owned by Franklin W. Olin. His son, John M. Olin, a hunter and shooter who became a force in American business, eventually took over Winchester-Western (as the company was known after

1935) and personally "adopted" the Model 21. Thanks to Olin, the 21 eventually achieved fame as the double gun for the affluent American shooter who demanded durability above all else. Model 21s differ in the quality of wood and the degree of engraving, but never by quality of construction or materials.

In its lifetime, the Model 21 was made in more than 27 grades ranging from plain field guns to incredibly ornate "Grand Royal" showpieces. (Seven of these were planned; only three were ever completed.) From 1930 to '40, the price of a standard M21 approximately doubled. But when production resumed after the Second World War, the price jumped to $185 in 1946 ($2,100 today) and thereafter costs rose steadily. With sales averaging fewer than a thousand a year, the Model 21 was trapped in an unprofitable limbo somewhere between low-price mass-production items and high-cost bespoke guns. In 1959 Winchester decided to offer the 21 on a made-to-order basis only and charge accordingly. By then, approximately 30,000 M21s had been made; by the time the Winchester Custom Shop closed, in 1993, a further thousand or so had been produced. In 1995 a small private enterprise called the Connecticut Shotgun Manufacturing Company bought the remaining Model 21 parts and the rights to make the gun again.

Book 8 of Abercrombie & Fitch's ledgers records the sale to Ernest Hemingway of Model 21 No. 15593 on 18 December 1940 for $117.30. It was a Skeet-grade 20-gauge with 26-inch barrels, choked Skeet #1 and Skeet #2. It had a full pistol grip, a beavertail forend and the standard single selective trigger, and it weighed 6 pounds 11 ounces. The stock had a length of pull—the distance from the trigger to the center of the buttplate—of 14⅜ inches and drops (measured from the extended line of the barrels to the top of the stock, fore and aft) of 1½ and 2³/₁₆ inches. It would have had the standard thin, hard-rubber buttplate.

Today No. 15593 has a soft, leather-covered recoil pad and its stock has been cut down to 13½ inches.

Earlier in 1940, however, Hemingway bought another 20-gauge Model 21, Serial Number 14267. Winchester's production records for No. 14267 are confusing. The original sheet—now part of the vast Winchester collection at the Cody Firearms Museum in Wyoming—was written over in some places and scratched out in others. Warren Newman, the Cody firearms curator, wrote in an e-mail, "As best I can interpret [the records], this firearm was originally manufactured on 2 January 1940. It must have come back to the factory on 10 December 1940, and gone out again on 25 January 1941.

"Hemingway's name is not in the records. The only contact data is 'Cia Piera Toras, Van Nusston, S.A.,' but we are unable to make any real sense of it."

The gun does not appear in Abercrombie & Fitch's books, so it was bought elsewhere—perhaps from another dealer or a private individual, perhaps even from the Sun Valley

Resort. (Was it the very gun Martha had done well with, loaned by Taylor Williams?) "Cia Piera Toras, Van Nusston, S.A." is a mystery as well.

Number 14267 is also a Skeet-grade gun with a single selective trigger and a beavertail forend. Today it has 28-inch barrels choked Full and Full and its length of pull is only $12^3/_4$ inches. The gun has a silver button set into the end of its grip on which are engraved the initials M.G.H.

Lloyd Arnold wrote that in November 1940 (a month before Hemingway bought No. 15593 from A&F) he saw in Ernest's gun rack at the Sun Valley Lodge a new Model 21 Winchester in 20 gauge—"his promised gift to Marty on her birthday"—with "an extra set of barrels for long-range work." [1] And M.G.H. is Martha Gellhorn Hemingway. Martha's birthday present is surely M21 No. 14267. It could have been sent back to New Haven in the following month to have the engraved silver escutcheon added or the stock shortened.

In the 67 years between the time Martha received the gun and it was sold to its present owner by James D. Julia Auctioneers, in October 2007, one set of barrels—the more open-choked barrels, suitable for upland birds in Idaho—has disappeared, leaving only the Full & Full set on the gun. Photos of long-legged Martha standing next to her six-foot husband indicate she was

*Cuba, circa 1942-'43. Patrick Hemingway, then 14 or 15, accepts what may be a shooting trophy, probably at the Club des Cazadores. His gun lacks the distinctive front and middle sight beads (on the rib between the barrels) of the family Model 21s.*

John F. Kennedy Library

a tall woman, and at least by modern standards a 12¾-inch stock seems short for her—but not for the next Mrs. Hemingway, a petite 5'2", who "inherited" it.

Ernest evidently bought Model 21 No. 15593 from Abercrombie & Fitch shortly after

*Idaho, 1946 or '47. Papa with his Winchester Model 12 and Mary Welsh Hemingway, his fourth wife. She appears to be carrying one of the family Model 21s. Martha, probably pleased to give up hunting when she and Ernest divorced, left her birthday shotgun behind.*

John F. Kennedy Library

otherwise have missed parts of two hunting seasons.

No. 15593 does not appear to have been Ernest's gun; except for his early 16-bore Browning A-5, his shotguns seem to have all been 12-gauges, and every side-by-side double gun in his hands in photographs looks to be his English W. & C. Scott.

Ernest's and Martha's marriage lasted five years. Next up, after Word War II, was Mary Welsh, another journalist, who became the fourth and final Mrs. Ernest Hemingway on 14 March 1946. Her indoctrination into shooting had begun the previous summer, in Cuba, when she wrote the lines at the top of

he'd gotten his wife's gun, No. 14267. If in fact he'd shipped her birthday gun to Winchester a week earlier, as the record suggests, No. 15593 could have been a replacement for her to use while hers was being modified. Since No. 14267 evidently was not shipped out again by Winchester until January 1941, she would

this chapter. Gigi—Ernest's youngest son, Gregory, just turned 17—offered to teach her to handle the Model 21: "bead on target, head down, stock firm at shoulder." He had her shoot at a cardboard box at different ranges, to show her how the shot pattern spread with distance; then came the daily flight of *negritos*,

*Winchester Model 21 No. 32447, a presentation-grade 12-gauge embellished by master engraver Nick Kusmit, was made for Hemingway when he was named the Winchester Outdoorsman of the Year for 1959. The gun still wasn't finished by the time of his death, in July 1961, so he never received it. Today it is displayed prominently in the entry to the main gallery of the Cody Firearms Museum at the Buffalo Bill Historic Center in Wyoming.*

small black birds that fed in the fields and returned to their roosts in the trees of Havana each evening. "Move with them and shoot," Gigi said, and demonstrated. With each shot a bird fell, some so far off that Mary thought they might have had heart attacks. When it was her turn, Mary fired and reloaded and fired again until the cartridges were gone— one bird down. Back at the house, Papa asked how she'd done. "Okay," Gigi replied. "Okay for a first go." [2]

Over time the two Model 21s, all but identical, became known in the family as "Mary's guns," and Mary herself became, in her husband's pronouncement, a "brilliant but erratic shot." She was always more comfortable shooting birds than four-legged game, and she shot the Model 21s far more than she did her Mannlicher-Schoenauer rifle. (After Ernest's death, she once ran off some unwelcome visitors to the Idaho house by firing one of her 21s at their car.) Mary continued to hunt after Ernest's death, sometimes with her friend Clara Spiegel in Idaho. She returned to East Africa in

1962 to go on safari with her stepson Patrick, and she hunted with *Sports Afield* columnist and trapshooting great Jimmy Robinson at his waterfowl lodge near Winnipeg, and with a young man from Southern California named Bruce Tebbe.

Tebbe was a friend of Denne Bart Petitclerc, the reporter-turned-scriptwriter who became a Hemingway friend and moved from California to Sun Valley. Petitclerc in turn introduced Tebbe to Mary Hemingway after Ernest's death, and the two of them often hunted together with the Model 21s. The 12th clause in the Last Will and Testament of Mary Hemingway, dated 26 October 1979, directed that when she died her two 20-gauge Model 21 Winchesters would go to Bruce Tebbe. He sold them in the late 1980s—to his regret, he said—and eventually, in October 2007, the two guns appeared in the same James D. Julia auction that offered Hemingway's Woodsman pistol No. 128866-S. The same bidder, a Michigan sportsman and Hemingway aficionado, bought all three.

# A Pair of Merkel
# Over/Unders & a Single

*The Scott and a very beautiful twenty-eight inch barrel over-and-under Merkel had fitted me and I had shot them both for many years.*

—*Under Kilimanjaro,* page 392

Among the most mysterious of Ernest Hemingway's guns is the German-made Merkel over/under he mentioned just once in his published writings, in an aside in *Under Kilimanjaro* (above) and referred to once in an unpublished letter. We have identified a Merkel shotgun in only one Hemingway photo as well. The gun—or rather guns—came to light almost accidentally.

The 14th clause of Mary Hemingway's 1979 will left "to Charles and Gioia Larkin of Gannet, Idaho, all other guns, shotguns and rifles wheresoever situated at the time of my death." (Other guns, that is, than her Model 21s and Mannlicher-Schoenauer rifle, which went to Bruce Tebbe and Bud Purdy.) The Larkins owned a ranch south of Sun Valley where Hemingway and the "tribe" often hunted. We learned that in the mid-1990s one of Charles Larkin's sons received from his father a 12-gauge Merkel over/under that was part of the Hemingway bequest. We also discovered that Papa had bought not one but two

Merkels, a secondhand matched pair, from Abercrombie & Fitch. Thus we made two assumptions, both incorrect: first, that the Larkin gun was one of them; and second, that the serial number of its mate would be one digit higher or lower.

However, the Larkin Merkel's serial number is 26724. The A&F ledger records that the pair of Merkels sold to "E. Hemingway" on 12 March 1945 were numbered 19342 and 19865. These guns were 12-gauges chambered for three-inch Magnum shells; each had two sets of barrels, 28 and 32 inches long, and adjustable combs and buttpads, and they had been built to an unusually high standard. A true pair in every respect save two, they had been consigned—along with three other unusual Merkel over/unders—to A&F by "W.G. Brokaw" in 1944. A year later, Papa paid $1,500 for them, equivalent to nearly $18,000 in 2010, making them the most costly guns that we know he owned. (A similar pair today would cost at least $60,000.)

In the spring of 1945 Hemingway had arrived in New York from Paris, at the close of the Second World War in Europe, and was revisiting his old haunts in the city with his middle son, Patrick, who was then just 16. On March 13, Hemingway wrote a long and loving letter to Mary Welsh, *Time* Magazine's war correspondent in London who would become his fourth wife, which includes this paragraph: "When found we had 20,000 C.O.H. [cash on hand] all debts paid I bought 2 shotguns as no sense going around . . . with no guns and have had no chance to buy anything for so long.

that the gun was not only very expensive but also, because of what he thought was shiny cadmium plating, downright ugly.

It is no surprise that Hemingway knew, or at least knew of, the original owner of the Merkel guns. William Gould Brokaw was a fabulously wealthy and high-profile "clubman," a New York socialite who favored country estates, racing yachts, blooded horses, airplanes and fast cars, as well as pigeon shooting and quail hunting. Naturally, he attracted women, and he was married three times; his entanglements and divorce proceedings were

*A representative, between-the-wars Merkel Model 303 "Luxus" over/under with hand-detacaable, Holland & Holland-style sidelocks, ejectors, a single selective trigger, a straight-grip stock and full-length forend, and an extra set of barrels. This one appears to be configured for shooting game, not as a competition gun.*                                    James D. Julia Auctioneers

. . . They were second hand and belonged to an old bastard I could always beat in old days but he had fanciest guns in the world and now he's dead and I have the guns. If can't shoot them we'll sell to some S.A. millionaire."

Hemingway probably meant one of the wealthy South Americans who also frequented the Club des Cazadores in Cuba. In the *Kansas City Star*, on 27 June 1999, Patrick recalled this visit to Abercrombie & Fitch with his father. However, he wrote of only one secondhand Merkel, not a pair, and commented

colorful, to say the least, and generated hundreds of breathless newspaper stories across America. Brokaw was born in 1863, the son of William Vail Brokaw, one of the successful Brokaw Brothers clothiers, themselves sons of railroad tycoon and "robber baron" Jay Gould. W.G. Brokaw reportedly inherited $4.5 million and never worked a day in his life, save for doing his best to spread his fortune by commissioning extravagant homes, boats, cars and guns, and backing companies that made some of these things. He cut a memo-

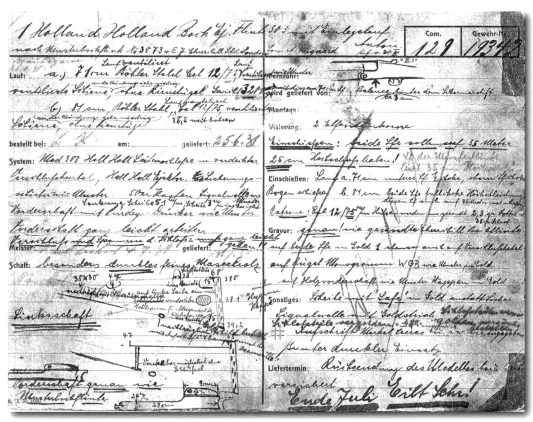

*Order card #129, for Merkel No. 19342, the first of two deluxe 12-gauge Model 303 over/unders, each with two sets of barrels chambered for three-inch Magnum cartridges, built "very much in a hurry" for W.G. Brokaw in 1931-'32. Stock dimensions are given in great detail. The gun was to place its shot pattern 25 centimetres high at 35 metres. The exhaustive specifications continue on the back, where there are scribbled calculations indicating that the gun would weigh 43 grams more with the longer barrels. Clearly, this was to be a dedicated, high-stakes competition gun.*

Merkel Jagd- und Sportwaffen

rable figure on Long Island, where the young F. Scott Fitzgerald (who became a friend and confidant of Hemingway) was growing up, and he may have been an inspiration for "the great Gatsby."

Around 1900, Brokaw built Fairview Lodge, a lavish house on his plantation near Trinity, North Carolina. By then he had traveled to London and become an aficionado of fine English shotguns. In 1898 he ordered

*Order card #292, for Merkel No. 19865, the second of the Brokaw/Hemingway matched pair—a Schwesterflinte, or "sister gun." It emphasizes that this gun must be exactly like the first one but notes that a consecutive serial number is not available. True matched pairs of guns are ordered at the same time and to identical specifications and are numbered sequentially; this then was a "composed" pair—the second gun completed 17 months after the first. Yet the first gun, No. 19342, was ordered with a gold-inlaid "1," indicating that Brokaw intended to order at least a No. 2 gun made to the same style and dimensions.* Merkel Jagd- und Sportwaffen

from E.J. Churchill (Gunmakers) Ltd. a 12-bore quail gun with barrels precisely 26$^{1}/_{16}$ inches long. Don Masters, who was associated with that company from 1958 into the 1990s and wrote *The House of Churchill*, identified

this as the forerunner of what would become Churchill's trademark short-barreled guns. (Most shotgun barrels are 28 to 30 inches long.) Thereafter, Gould and his friend Clarence Mackay, another American millionaire

— 53 —

sportsman, ordered a number of such guns (which typically cost about a year's wages for a working man). Robert Churchill was a teenager then and evidently paying attention; after he took over the family firm he made his name in part by developing a style of game shooting around a line of uniquely short-barreled guns. Between the wars, Churchill's various "XXV" models—which had, naturally, 25-inch tubes—became well known on the grouse moors of Northumberland and Scotland. In the right hands, a compact, quick-handling gun proved to be as effective on fast, elusive red grouse as it was on fast, elusive American quail.

Brokaw's early impact on Churchill was, 30 years later, reflected back in the pair of Merkels that would wind up with Ernest Hemingway. The Churchill order books indicate that in the 1920s Brokaw switched from buying side-by-side shotguns to over/unders. This could have been driven by an interest in shooting targets, especially boxed pigeons, instead of game. Competition shotgunners, who have time to prepare for their targets, usually prefer the narrower, more precise (or less obtrusive) sighting plane of a single barrel on top. Robert Churchill, a renowned pigeon shot with a side-by-side, dismissed the over/under gun as a "fad or novelty" but knew that if he didn't give his clients what they wanted, they'd go elsewhere. According to Don Masters, Churchill borrowed the finer points of both the Boss and Woodward designs to create his Premiere over/under. Only some 40 of these shotguns were ever made, of which five

were commissioned by W. Gould Brokaw—but the last two orders, placed in 1931, were cancelled. Something diverted Brokaw from Churchill's English over/unders to Merkels, made in Germany.

The first of Brokaw's deluxe Merkel over/unders, No. 19342, was completed on 25 June 1931, and its *Schwesterflinte*, or "sister gun," on 12 December 1932. Einar Hoff, of Merkel USA, unearthed the production cards from the factory records in Suhl. These were in German, translated for us by Dietrich Apel, founder of the German Gun Collectors Association. Apel called the instructions for these two Merkels—highly customized 12-gauge Model 303 over/unders with detachable ("Holland & Holland") sidelocks—the most extensive he has ever seen. Details included the exact slope of the ribs, gold-plated lockwork, a coat of arms inlaid in each forend, and a balance point three centimeters behind the hinge pin. The first gun had a gold "1" on the breech—a strong indication that it was meant to be one of at least a pair, even though there was a delay (in time and serial numbers, the two ways in which they differ from a true pair) in building the second gun. And finally, a Churchill Premiere was provided to Merkel to serve as a model for the engraving!

In the small city of Suhl, where German gunmaking began in the 16th Century, the firm of Gebrüder Merkel (Merkel Bros.) is a relative newcomer. However the brothers—Albert, Gebhard, Karl and Oskar—came from a long line of gunsmiths, stockmakers and engravers, and the family name was well known in town. On 1 September 1898, these four founded a trading company "for the purpose of joint manufacture of firearms and other articles." Their objective was, and has remained, the manufacture of hunting, target and "luxury" guns. The brothers built multi-barrel and single-shot guns, as well as heavy double rifles in traditional British calibers such as .475 No. 2 and .500 and .577 Nitro Express, but from the start Merkel specialized in over/unders.

A decade after Gebrüder Merkel was established, modern break-action shotguns with their barrels stacked one atop the other were beginning to appear in England, courtesy of Boss and Woodward. In Germany, however, the over/under dates back almost 400 years earlier, to the days of the wheellock gun, and then to the flintlock *Wender*, or turn-over gun—an over/under whose barrels could be rotated, by hand, to bring each one into alignment with the single, top-mounted firing mechanism.

These were muzzleloading guns; when reliable breechloaders arrived, in the mid-1800s, a unique tradition of building multi-barreled guns evolved in Germany. *Drilling* (three-barrel) and even *Vierling* (four-barrel) guns became common, in every possible combination—two shotgun tubes with a rifle barrel underneath, two rifle barrels with a shotgun barrel beneath, over/under shotgun barrels with a rifle alongside, or two of each in a diamond cluster. The various barrels are chambered for two or even three different calibers and gauges. The result is a

versatile, if sometimes slightly clumsy (not to say confusing) hunting arm that may suit game from partridge to stag by way of fox, capercaille and boar. More than most German gunmakers, however, Gebrüder Merkel was influenced by British gun design and chose to concentrate on *Querflinte* (side-by-side) and especially *Bockflinte* (over/under) guns with only two barrels.

Most such Merkels use an immensely strong locking mechanism patented in England in 1873, the Greener crossbolt. Over/under Merkels use a variation of it known as the Kersten *Verschluss*, developed by a Prussian military armorer named Gustav Kersten. Greener extended the rib between the side-by-side barrels of his guns into a lug that, when the gun is closed, fits into a slot in the standing breech; a bar inside the action body, actuated by the toplever, slides laterally into a hole in this extension, pinning it securely. An over/under gun, with its stacked barrels, has two lugs, one on each side of the top tube, and this was Kersten's evolution. The British gun trade almost unanimously ignored its countryman's invention, but the crossbolt evidently suited Merkel's fail-safe approach to engineering. One of Merkel's side-by-side guns, the Model 124, is virtually a copy of a Greener in style and features. (W.W. Greener, famously quarrelsome and opinionated, may have irritated his peers at home to the point that few English gunmakers wanted anything to do with his inventions.)

Merkel relied heavily on foreign sales. Predictably, the First World War resulted in the loss of many markets. Nevertheless, the company was back in full operation by 1924 and was soon exporting to 28 countries. Gebrüder Merkel's reputation for strength and quality drew orders from European and Indian royalty, heads of state and industrial magnates, and serious shooters such as William Gould Brokaw. One prominent client was Max Schmeling, the world heavyweight boxing champion from 1930 to '32. Merkel guns were awarded the Grand Prix at the Paris World Exhibition of 1937. Merkel catalogs of the 1930s are in English, French, Spanish and Italian, as well as German.

Even during the two world wars that devastated Europe and then after Suhl disappeared behind the Iron Curtain in 1945, Merkel never produced military arms. As the Second World War approached, Hitler's government ordered Merkel to produce parts for engines and rangefinders, and carbines made by others. The city of Suhl largely escaped Allied bombing and, perhaps because Merkel hadn't made weapons during the war, the Soviet occupiers allowed the company to keep its machine tools. As a result, while much of urban and industrial Germany was still a smoking ruin at the end of 1945, Merkel Bros. was able to resume the production of sporting arms almost immediately. However, Suhl was now in the Deutsche Demokratische Republik, so instead of selling on the open market, Merkel was forced to send many of its guns to other Soviet Bloc countries as part of Germany's war-reparation payments. Eventually Merkel became a Communist state-owned

"showcase company" that made presentation guns for seemingly every friend of the USSR, including Nikita Khrushchev, Marshall Tito, Gamal Abdel Nasser, Yuri Gagarin and Mao Tse Tung. Even Dwight Eisenhower was presented with a Merkel. Between 1945 and 1987, Merkel reportedly produced 150,000 over/under guns alone.

The Berlin Wall fell in 1989; East and West Germany were reunited. The years that followed were difficult, as the loss of government support meant that Merkel (among many other firms) had to return to free-market capitalism not only to survive but also to replace its 1950s manufacturing technology. Once again, Merkel rebuilt itself, as Merkel Jagd- und Sportwaffen GmbH, while searching for new business.

Today the company has 200 employees and exports to more than 40 countries; in June 2007 it was acquired by a holding company based in Abu Dhabi. In the mid-1990s all Merkel guns underwent thorough re-engineering and they now represent a blend of traditional handcraftsmanship and modern computer-controlled machining. It is a tribute to Merkel's original designs, however, that a Model 303 over/under made today differs mechanically only in minor details from the guns that William Gould Brokaw ordered 80 years ago.

Suhl itself is now thriving again as well. In the central square stands a monument to the city's gunmakers that was erected in 1903. After a half-century of denying its heritage, the city decided to re-embrace its rich gunmak-

*At the Finca Vigía, late 1940s; the only photo yet found of the mysterious Merkel(s). Hemingway shows an American Army Sergeant First Class what is surely one of the pair of Merkel over/under shotguns that had been made for W. Gould Brokaw in 1931-'32. Note the Kersten fastener extending from the breech. The high ventilated rib on the top barrel and the lightweight cutaway forend are characteristic of competition guns. Under extreme magnification, it is possible to make out the line of the adjustable comb in the buttstock. The unusual silvery finish of both barrels and action, which Patrick Hemingway thought was cadmium plating, is another mystery; according to the order cards, Brokaw wanted dark color-case-hardened receivers. (Despite gates and signs reading "Visitors received ONLY by appointment," American tourists in Cuba thought nothing of barging in on the Hemingways; Ernest, however, had a soft spot for servicemen and often invited them in.)* John F. Kennedy Library

ing history and in 2008 Suhl dedicated its restored and expanded arms museum.

Brokaw eventually owned at least five Merkel over/unders, as that is how many were sent to Abercrombie & Fitch in June 1944 for sale in his name. Brokaw died in February 1941, so the guns must have been consigned by his son (who, by the way, continued to order Churchills) or a trustee. None sold until 1945, when the war ended. Only one of the five, a 12-gauge, had just one set of barrels; and not only are the barrels short, just 25½ inches long, but the gun was also chambered for everyday 2¾-inch cartridges. The serial number of this gun, 19827, dates it between the two that Hemingway bought and makes it Brokaw's second Merkel. It seems that Brokaw was replicating the style of his Churchill quail guns in an over/under Merkel while trying his first Merkel competition gun, No. 19342, in the pigeon ring. He must have approved of it, for its mate, No. 19865, followed a year and a half later.

(The two other consigned Brokaw Merkels were both 10-gauge guns, one with two and the other with three sets of barrels—26, 26 and 29 inches long, all choked differently. These would have been field guns also, as 10-bores are not allowed in competition.)

Only Hemingway's two Brokaw guns appear to have been a matched pair. Their 15-inch lengths of pull would have suited a shooter of Hemingway's size, but the Merkel work cards note that these guns were "cast on [bent slightly] for a left-handed shooter"—which Papa was not. He could have had the stocks "cast off," or bent in the other direction—or, since they appear in no known photos at the Club des Cazadores, he may have decided early on that he didn't like them after all and did

indeed sell them to "some S.A. millionaire." In any event, these exceptional guns seem to have disappeared.

The single Larkin Merkel, No. 26724, is a different shotgun entirely, a less-expensive boxlock (not the more complex sidelock) type. Its factory work card indicates that it was shipped in 1940, but a mystery attaches to this shotgun also: It has *two* work cards—one dated 7 August 1939 for a 12-gauge Model 400E, with metric dimensions carefully noted for a pistol-grip-type stock with a cheekpiece, and the other for a Model 401E, a mechanically identical gun, also in 12 gauge with 72cm (28-inch, approximately) barrels and 70mm (2¾-inch) chambers, but with game-scene engraving, an eye for a carrying sling soldered to the bottom barrel, an ivory-bead front sight, and a straight-grip stock of different dimensions and with no cheekpiece. This second order is dated 31 December 1939. The same serial number was applied to both.

Apparently Model 400E No. 26724 was not built, or at least not completed; the order was changed in December and the resultant 401E shotgun was then delivered on 6 July 1940 to the Magdeburg office of Waffen-Loesche, a German distributor of sporting goods. The Second World War had engulfed Europe by then, so exports to the US were no more. How and when this gun made its way out of Germany and into Hemingway's hands in Idaho is not known. It may have been one of the many fine sporting guns "liberated"—or bought legitimately—by American servicemen and brought home after the war. Probably not by Hemingway, though, for his March 13 letter to Mary seems to say that he had no guns with him when he arrived in New York.

Except for a rubber recoil pad, which could have been added any time, the Larkin Merkel, Serial No. 26724, fits the work order for the Model 401E of that number, from the engraving and the straight-grip stock to the sling eye. With its 72cm barrels, it could be the "very beautiful 28-inch over-and-under Merkel" that Hemingway mentioned in *Under Kilimanjaro.* Indeed, if Hemingway did sell the Brokaw pair in Cuba—he would not have shot well with guns built for a left-hander—then he most likely was referring to what is now Larkin's Merkel.

According to Sean Larkin, his mother Gioia and Mary Hemingway became close friends and spent much time together after Ernest's death. Mary died in 1986, Gioia in 1990 and Charles Larkin in 2009. Save for this Merkel, which Charles gave to his son Sean, whatever other guns were in Mary's bequest are so far unaccounted for.

There is one more twist to this story, another of the half-ironic, half-incredible coincidences that seem to stick to the Hemingway narrative like cosmic cockleburs: On his mother's side Sean Larkin is a great-great-grandson of Jay Gould—grandfather of W.G. Brokaw, who commissioned the other Hemingway Merkels.

# THE BERETTA S3 OVER/UNDER

*A Beretta over/under shotgun, Model S3, that was purchased in Venice . . . by Papa Hemingway.* —Mapes Auction Gallery catalog, October 1999

Even what seems to be a relatively well-documented Hemingway gun can lead to confusion. Firearms authority R.L. Wilson's book *The World of Beretta* mentions that Papa bought a 12-gauge Beretta SO3 over/under, No. 5991, in Venice in December 1949. Mary Hemingway's memoir, backed up by letters from Ernest, recalls that in the fall of 1948 he was hunting ducks in the lagoons of Venice with a new shotgun. Beretta, however, claims that Hemingway bought the gun at Armeria Caccia, a hunting store on Venice's Via San Marco, on 2 December 1947—or was it instead shipped from the factory in nearby Val Trompia to the shop on that date? The serial number and proof marks dates its manufacture to 1947. Furthermore, the gun is marked "S3," not "SO3."

The accepted Hemingway chronology puts the man in Idaho in October, November and December of 1947 (working on *Islands in the Stream* while Taylor Williams introduced Mary to big-game hunting) and in Venice for many weeks in the autumn of 1948 and again in the winter of 1949-'50. Duck hunting figures prominently in both years in Italy, but new guns appear in the memoirs and letters only in 1948, and no makers' names are mentioned.

Was the "new gun" that Papa used for duck hunting with Baron Nanyuki Franchetti in 1948, when he joked that he'd been "shooting in a Venetian blind,"[1] the W. & C. Scott—or was it this Beretta? The Armeria Caccia aside, could the Beretta have been bought alongside the Scott, from the dealer from Udine who brought guns to the Kechlers' villa in Codroipo in the fall of '48?[2] Or did he buy the Scott in '48 and the Beretta in 1949? In any event, we have found nothing in any Hemingway narratives or letters that points specifically to the Beretta.

To date, much of what is known about this gun comes from one famous photograph and from Book 19, page 306, of the Abercrombie & Fitch gun ledgers, which records that on 3 July 1963 "E. Hemingway"—i.e., Mary, almost exactly two years post Ernest's death—consigned Beretta No. 5991 to A&F for sale. The date agrees with the consignment of three other important Hemingway guns: a Winchester Model 61 .22 rifle, his Winchester Model 12 No. 525488 and the Griffin & Howe

Springfield. A month later, on August 9, a man named Cy Mueller bought Papa's Beretta for $250, of which Mary received $125.

(The A&F records are a unique window on American society. On the same day, 9 August 1963, Abercrombie & Fitch sold a matched pair of Jos. Lang guns that had been consigned by Bernard Baruch, the financier and statesman. Those guns brought $4,500; Baruch netted $3,000.)

In somewhat sloppy handwriting, an A&F employee described the Beretta as a 12-gauge over/under, no model name or number giv-

hard leather leg-o'-mutton case stamped with Hemingway's name and Cuban address.

It would be nearly impossible for Ernest Hemingway, an ardent hunter and shooter who favored double guns and who spent so much time in northern Italy, *not* to have acquired a Beretta somewhere along the way.

Between Milan and Venice lies the city of Brescia—equally ancient and historic, if less glamorous and less well known outside Italy. Brescia is on the Mella River at the mouth of Val Trompia, a valley that funnels south-

*Beretta S3 No. 5991, a 12-gauge sidelock gun with double triggers and 70cm (approximately 27½-inch) barrels choked Modified & Full. The ungainly recoil pad is a later addition. The Monobloc seam in the barrels is clearly visible, just above the beginning of the forend wood. Ernest Hemingway bought this elegant gun on one of his lengthy visits to northern Italy in the fall of 1948 or '49. How much he paid for it is not known, but in August 1963, two years after his death, Abercrombie & Fitch sold it for $250. The gun changed hands once more, and then Beretta USA's Peter Horn bought it for his employer, at auction in October 1999, for $71,500. Beretta has turned down offers of as much as $200,000 for it.*

Terry Allen

en, weighing seven pounds, in a "fleese" case, with 27½-inch barrels choked Full/Full and 2¾-inch chambers. "Full & Full" is an unusual choke arrangement; Beretta now lists the chokes as Modified and Full, which is more normal. And rather than a fleece case, a description that calls to mind a full-length, zippered leather or cloth sleeve, when Beretta re-acquired the gun, in 1999, it was in a

ward out of the Pre-Alps. The region was rich in iron and timber, and its mountain streams provided power. The critical third ingredient was the inhabitants themselves—clever, hard-working artisans and entrepreneurs with a gift for working metal. From this mix emerged in the Middle Ages what may have been the world's earliest industrial district. From the beginning its primary product was arms.

It began with edged weapons and armor, and then crossbows. Then the mechanics of Val Trompia made their lasting mark: Some historians credit them with inventing portable firearms—possibly first used in battle in 1282, when the city of Forli, southeast of Brescia, was besieged by a French force under the command of Pope Martin IV. With the development of "hand cannons" came a parallel evolution of manufacturing technology. By 1509, Pietro Francino di Gardone had built a water-powered forge that could pound out 10 barrel blanks per day. While England's Industrial Revolution was being delayed for two centuries by Henry VIII's destruction of the iron-ore smelter at Rievaulx Abbey in 1538, in Val Trompia the production of gun barrels had been broken down into nine steps, with trained specialists carrying out each one. In 1562 the mayor of Brescia reported that the valley had produced some 25,000 guns that year. In 1804 one in three of the region's population was in the arms trade.

Brescia now makes auto parts and machine tools, but the flagship industry of Gardone, Marcheno and Sarezzo, the towns that lie farther up in Val Trompia, continues to be firearms. In this tangle of winding streets and modest stone and stucco buildings, every kind of sporting gun is made, from target pistols to reproductions of historic muzzleloaders to big-game rifles, and of course shotguns. According to the chamber of commerce, there are more than 150 companies in the valley engaged in some aspect of building guns. Virtually all of them are family enterprises; some are individual craftsmen; many are tiny boutique firms with a handful of employees. One of them, however, is a privately held, multinational conglomerate that is recognized as the oldest industrial firm in existence: Fabbrica d'Armi Pietro Beretta S.p.A.

Today the Beretta family's ancestral home in Gardone is nearly hidden among slightly grimy industrial buildings. Nearby is the company's headquarters and private museum. In the files is a receipt from the office of the Doge of Venice that translates as follows:

"On this, the 3rd day of October 1526. [To] Master Bartolomeo Beretta of the Brescian territory of Gardone for 185 arquebus barrels [made] for our House of the Arsenal [is given] 296 ducats."

Beretta refers to this document—there are three more original copies of it in the archives of Venice—as its birth certificate. During the intervening five centuries, *maestro da canne* (master barrelmaker) Bartolomeo's foundry has grown into one of the most technologically sophisticated and successful makers of sporting, police and military firearms in the world. The modern firm's name honors Pietro Beretta, born in 1791, because it was he who launched its aggressive expansion, which his son Giuseppe continued by opening up export markets. In 1988, not long after winning the milestone contract to supply the US Army with a new pistol to replace the Colt Model 1911, Dr. Pier Giuseppe Beretta noted that his family company had managed to survive and prosper for nearly 500 years because "we have always lived in Gardone, in intimate contact with its people, working at a trade which we have always loved . . . . Cut off from the distractions of city life, we have concentrated on only one thing: Making guns."

Sixteen generations of Berettas have been active in the company, which is currently managed by Ugo Gussalli Beretta and his sons Pietro and Franco. Today, when most of the world's other historic gunmaking centers—including Birmingham, in England; Liège, in Belgium; St. Etienne, France; and Hartford, Connecticut—have diversified into other industries, Val Trompia remains a hothouse of gunmaking skills and personalities. Among its former client states, Venice now relies on tourism and Milan is "la moda" and the opera; in the valley, the art, science and business of building guns goes on.

A fter the Second World War, Beretta's output of sporting shotguns shifted to over/unders. The *Sovrapposto*, Beretta's answer to John Browning's Superposed of 1930, made its public debut in 1933 or '34. The 1935 Beretta catalog listed three versions: S.01 and S.02 "Super Hunter" models and an S.03 "Super *Tiro*" competition gun, all in 12 gauge and "patented 1934." The more lavishly engraved S.02's list price was 2,650 lira, officially equivalent then to $140. That was about 40 percent more than a Browning, but a buyer with cash US dollars could probably have gotten a much better black-market price in Italy at the time. (This would have been even more so in late-'40s, post-war Italy, when Hemingway bought his S3.)

BREVATTO—"patented." Ernest Hemingway's S3, made soon after the Second World War, was an evolution of Beretta's first modern over/under gun, the S.01, which appeared in 1933. "S" is for sovrapposto—"superposed," or over/under—and the numbers 01, 02, 03 apparently designated the first versions. In the mid- or late 1950s the numeral 0 was dropped and the letter O was added, perhaps for "Special Order." The resultant SO series are Beretta's premium-grade sidelock shotguns, all over/unders. Along with guns marked S1, S2 and S3, there have been SO1, SO2, SO3, SSO4, SO5, SO6 and SO9 models, with variations designated EL and EELL. Today Beretta's top-of-the-line shotgun is the SO10, which begins at well over $100,000.                    Terry Allen

Beretta's 1938 catalog explained, in literally translated English, that the company's designers had found solutions to the "problems" of over/unders made by "the best known foreign factories." Instead of a full-width hinge beneath the action, Beretta let its barrels pivot on pins set into the sides of the action body and adopted the Kersten *Verschluss* from Germany, which put the locking lugs in line with the top barrel instead of under the bottom one. The result was a shotgun action that was both as streamlined as the Boss and as strong as the Merkel. This amounted to just common-sense applications of sound existing technology to suit the Italian design esthetic, but Beretta went a step further and refined a barrel-jointing technique patented in 1881 by a Belgian named Henri Pieper. With Beretta's marketing might behind it, this would now reverberate through the gunmaking world just as loudly as Anson & Deeley's English action patent did in 1875 (see "The .577 Nitro Express").

Instead of building pairs of barrels by painstakingly aligning and soldering two tubes to each other and then machining the hinge and latch surfaces into their breech ends, as everyone else did, Pieper fabricated the breech portion first, out of a block of steel, and then simply screwed the barrel tubes into sockets threaded into the block. By 1913 Beretta had adopted this method but was soldering thin-walled tubes into the block instead of using Pieper's screw threads. This reduced bulk and weight. Beretta then also added the ejector mechanisms to the block, another step that simplified the manufacture.

In the late 1920s or early '30s, when developing its first breechloading *sovrapposto* guns, Beretta used this so-called Monobloc technique. It was widely adopted in Val Trompia and eventually elsewhere, and one of the characteristics of Italian double guns is often a telltale seam in the barrels—usually decorated with a ring of engraving—just forward of the hinge pin, where the ends of the tubes butt up against the block. Italian makers of bespoke guns now offer their clients the choice of Monobloc or the more expensive traditional barrels, with seamless tubes (called "Demibloc" in Europe), but Ernest Hemingway's S3, a top-of-the-line model in its day, has this distinctive line.

Although their prices were far closer to the boxlock Browning Superposed made in Belgium than to the sidelock Boss- and Woodward-type guns from London, S-series Berettas from the beginning were built with sidelock actions. ("Lock" here means the mechanism by which a gun fires its ammunition, not how the action is fastened shut.) Each lock—the arrangement of cams, sears, springs and tumbler that detonates the cartridge—of a sidelock gun is mounted on a long oval plate inletted into the side of the stock at its head, where it meets the body of the gun. This is regarded as more esthetically pleasing than the simpler boxlock action, which contains its firing apparatus in a squared-off action "box" between the buttstock and barrels. A sidelock has some theoretical advantages in the geometry of its trigger linkage, and its sideplates offer a larger "canvas" for engraving; a boxlock is less complex and stronger but can look

*The Hemingway S3's rectangular Kersten-style locking bolt, here protruding from the side of the standing breech, is virtually invisible when the gun is closed. Note the distinctive long oval shape of the action's sidelock plates. The Spanish misspellings and omissions may be because the case was made in Italy; Hemingway's home was the Finca Vigía, "Lookout Manor," and it was in a village near Havana called San Francisco de Paula. "CCC" stands for Club des Cazadores del Cerro, the "club for shooters on the hill," where Hemingway was a member.* Terry Allen

chunky, especially when it has been designed for mass production.

The only way to sharply reduce the cost of an over/under gun is to industrialize it, which demands both a boxlock action and Monobloc barrels. This brings up an interesting question: Why did John Browning, in designing his Superposed—the over/under that would be built in huge numbers by Fabrique Nationale in Belgium—not also adopt Henri Pieper's barrelmaking technique as a way to reduce his gun's cost still further? Browning surely knew of it, for although Pieper's name is forgotten today, he was not an obscure gunmaker whose legacy was taken over by giant Beretta; in addition to building many guns under the trade name Bayard, he was a founding partner of another gunmaking giant: Fabrique Nationale itself.

At the 1964 Olympics an Italian named Ennio Matterelli won the gold medal in trapshooting with an over/under gun made in Italy by Daniele Perazzi. The shooting world, and in particular America, took notice, and Beretta was positioned to take advantage of this promotional coup. Today the company's mass-produced over/unders dominate their market worldwide, while its limited-production bespoke over/unders command huge prices. Modern Italian gunmakers, to a man (and woman), hold England's great houses—Purdey, Boss, Holland & Holland, Greener, Westley Richards, et al.—in the highest esteem for their side-by-side guns, but with the next breath proudly point to their own over/unders as the finest of their kind. Italy has refined the

over/under shotgun to a standard found nowhere else, and Beretta makes this tradition accessible to shooters of all pocketbooks.

In its catalog for the sale of 15 October 1999, when Beretta S3 No. 5991 went under the gavel, Mapes Auction Gallery noted that the gun and "about 17 or 18 others remained in Africa until 1964 when they were shipped to Abercrombie & Fitch Co., New York, to be offered for sale by Mary Hemingway."

In 1964 Mary recalled that she and Ernest had 18 to 20 guns on their 1953-'54 safari, but we are certain of only eight of them: the Model 12 and W. & C. Scott shotguns; the G&H, Model 61, Mannlicher and Westley Richards rifles; and probably two Woodsman pistols. It is true that Papa and Mary left Kenya without their guns (at least some of them) after that safari. Ernest, already battered from two bush-plane wrecks on the 23rd and 24th of January, compounded his injuries by falling into a brush fire while recuperating at a beach cottage at Shimoni, 50 miles south of Mombasa. Less than a week later, with Ernest all but invalided, Mary bundled him aboard the SS *Africa* for Venice by way of Port Said. There was no opportunity to pack properly and make all of the planned goodbyes. Five or six months later, when the Hemingways were at home in Cuba, arrived a letter from their friend William Hale, head of the Kenya Game Department. Along with reminding them that they owed the equivalent of $58.57 for extra game they had shot, Hale wrote that he had deposited Ernest's guns in the bank for safekeeping. (Denis Zaphiro had

*Cuba, 1948 or '49. Hemingway with his Beretta at the Club des Cazadores. The man may be a "trapper," whose job it was to spring the pigeons from their boxes at random. The bird boy collected the bag of pigeons. Since Papa's Springfield rifle, his Model 12 Winchester and Browning Superposed shotguns, and his original Colt Woodsman pistol have disappeared, the Beretta S3 has assumed pride of place as the most famous of his surviving guns—largely because of this photograph.* Roberto Herrera Sotolongo

probably taken charge of them after the Hemingways' disorganized departure, and then handed them off to his boss, Hale.) However, the guns were returned long before 1964: Arnold wrote of seeing the Model 12 in 1958; Papa probably put the Scott to deadly use in July 1961; and Mary consigned two of the known safari guns to Abercrombie & Fitch for sale in 1963. Of this Beretta, also consigned, we have found no indication, written or photographic, that it was taken on safari.

The Mapes catalog also mentions a letter from A&F, dated 5 March 1964, "verifying that this shotgun, serial number 5991, did indeed belong to Ernest Hemingway." The letter seems to have vanished; neither Mapes nor Beretta have it, and there is no copy in the Abercrombie & Fitch records. The gun, however, is now on display at the Beretta Gallery at 718 Madison Avenue in New York City.

# THE GRIFFIN & HOWE
# .30-06 SPRINGFIELD

*The Springfield finally came and you ought to see it kid.*

—to Mike Strater, late June 1930, while Hemingway was in Key West

M'Cola put the Springfield in my hand and I opened it to make sure I had solids. The rhino was out of sight now but I could see the shaking of the high grass.

"How far would you call it?"

"All of three hundred."

"I'll bust the son of a bitch."

I was watching, freezing myself deliberately inside, stopping the excitement as you close a valve, going into that impersonal state you shoot from.

He slowed, trotting into the shallow, boulder-filled stream. Thinking of one thing, that the shot was perfectly possible, but that I must lead him enough, must get ahead, I got on him, then well ahead of him, and squeezed off. I heard the whonk of the bullet and, from his trot, he seemed to explode forward. With a whooshing snort he smashed ahead, splashing water and snorting. I shot again and raised a little column of water behind him and shot again as he went into the grass; behind him again.

"Piga,' M'Cola said. "Piga!"

Droopy agreed.

"Did you hit him?" Pop said.

"Absolutely," I said. "I think I've got him."

Droopy was running and I re-loaded and ran off after him. Half the camp was strung out across the hills and waving and yelling. The rhino had come in right below where they were and gone up the valley toward where the forest came close to the head of the valley.

Pop and P.O.M. came up. Pop with his big gun and M'Cola carrying mine.

"Droopy will get the tracks," Pop said. "M'Cola swears you hit him."

"Piga!" M'Cola said.

"He snorted like a steam engine," P.O.M. said. "Didn't he look wonderful going along there?"

"He was late getting home with the milk," Pop said. "Are you sure you hit him? It was a godawful long shot."

"I know I hit him. I'm pretty sure I've killed him."

"Don't tell any one if you did," Pop said. "They'll never believe you. Look! Droopy's got blood."

Below, in the high grass, Droop was holding up grass blades towards us. Then, stooped, he went on trailing fast by the blood spoor.

*"Piga," M'Cola said. "M'uzuri!"*

*"We'll keep up above where we can see if he makes a break," Pop said. "Look at Droopy."*

*Droop had removed his fez and held it in his hands.*

*"That's all the precautions he needs," Pop said. "We bring up a couple of heavy guns and Droopy goes in after him with one article less of clothing."*

*Below us Droopy and his partner who was trailing with him had stopped. Droopy held up his hand.*

*"They hear him," Pop said. "Come on."*

*We started toward them. Droopy came toward us and spoke to Pop.*

*"He's in there," Pop whispered. "They can hear the tick birds. One of the boys said he heard the faro, too. We'll go in against the wind. You go ahead with Droopy. Let the Memsahib stay behind with me. Take the big gun. All right."*

*The rhino was in high grass, somewhere in there behind some bushes. As we went forward we heard a deep, moaning sort of groan. Droopy looked around at me and grinned. The noise came again, ending this time like a blood-soaked sigh. Droopy was laughing. "Faro," he whispered and put his hand palm open on the side of his head in the gesture that means to go to sleep. Then in a jerky-flighted, sharp-beaked little flock we saw the tick birds rise and fly away. We knew where he was and, as we went slowly forward, parting the high grass, we saw him. He was on his side, dead.*

*"Better shoot him once to make sure," Pop said. M'Cola handed me the Springfield he had been carrying. I noticed it was cocked, looked at M'Cola, furious with him, kneeled down and shot the rhino in the sticking place. He never moved. Droopy shook my hand and so did M'Cola.*

*"He had that damned Springfield cocked," I said to Pop. The cocked gun behind my back made me black angry.* (*Green Hills of Africa*, pages 68-70)

By the middle of the 20th Century, the .30-06 had become the most popular hunting cartridge in North America, if not the world. It was first used in a US military rifle called the Springfield, for the government armory where it was developed, in Springfield, Massachusetts. Ernest Hemingway's .30-06 was one of these, albeit much modified. He fell in love with it (the letter to Mike Strater,

*Hemingway's bolt-action .30-06, Serial No. 956, built by Griffin & Howe in 1930 on a Springfield barreled action bought through the NRA and selected by Col. Townsend Whelen, was very similar to this rifle. Including a side-mounted detachable telescopic sight, a sling and a leather case, the tab came to $256.50. Hemingway would soon remove the scope and never use it again.*

James D. Julia Auctioneers

above, continues: "[It] Comes up as naturally as pointing your finger . . . most beautifully made and finished and simple, practical gun I've ever seen." [1]) and used it extensively, in Montana, Wyoming and Idaho and on both of his East African safaris. Alongside his Model 12, it stayed with him all his life and became, in Lloyd Arnold's words, "the patinaed,

*The first Hemingway safari, Tanganyika, February 1934. From left: Ben Fourie, the camp's mechanic and driver; Ernest's Key West friend Charles Thompson, "Karl" in* Green Hills of Africa; *Philip Percival; and Hemingway pose with trophies—three kudu and an East African oryx. Percival, the very model of a laconic, dryly British gentleman and white hunter, impressed Hemingway tremendously. As "J.P."—"Jackson Phillips"—or "Pop" he became a central figure in the book. When Ernest returned to East Africa in 1953 for his second safari, Percival was persuaded to come out of retirement and once again become Pop, this time in* Under Kilimanjaro *and then* True at First Light.

Percival, born in 1886 in the north of England, emigrated to Kenya in 1906 at the urging of his older brother Blayney, who was a collector for the British Museum and became East Africa's first game warden. Philip set out to raise ostriches for the ladies' hat market, which shortly made him an expert in dealing with lions, who couldn't resist such easy pickings. At 23 he was tapped to join Theodore Roosevelt's 11-month safari as a junior hunter. He impressed the former President also: "At Bondoni was Percival, a tall sinewy man, a fine rider and shot . . . . I shall not soon forget seeing him one day, as he walked beside his twelve-ox

mellow-with-use gun—the one that Ernest really cared for, personally, above others."

The round eventually created for the Springfield was designated "Cartridge, Ball, Caliber .30, Model of 1906," hence .30-06. (It is sometimes referred to as the .30 Government also.) Just as its rifle was based on the German Mauser design, the .30-06 cartridge was derived from the 7.92x57mm round developed for the German commission rifle of 1888. In dozens of variations ranging from ordinary "ball" to armor-piercing and tracer, the .30-06 was so effective that it survived the US Army's transition from the bolt-action rifles of the First World War to the semi-automatic M1 Garand rifle of World War II and Korea. It also served brilliantly in full-automatic weapons such as the BAR (the Browning Automatic Rifle) and many tripod-, vehicle- and aircraft-mounted machine guns up until about 1970. By military standards, however, the .30-06 is a relatively large, powerful round that generates considerable recoil and demands a fairly heavy rifle. In the late 1950s US forces began a slow shift to smaller cartridges in lighter assault rifles capable of both semi- and full-automatic fire. By then, though, two generations of American soldiers had been indoctrinated in shooting the .30-06; when the Doughboys and GIs returned to hunting, it was with the beloved "aught-six."

But mere familiarity and numbers alone didn't make the .30-06 the top general-purpose hunting caliber; it took the right bullets to make it so extraordinarily versatile and effective on game. Military ammunition is rarely ideal for hunting. The Hague Convention of 1899 prohibited "the use of bullets which expand or flatten easily in the human body." Ever since, military bullets have been full-metal-jacketed types meant to leave behind fairly clean, one-diameter

---

*team, cracking his long whip, while in the big wagon sat pretty Mrs. Percival with a puppy, and a little cheetah cub, which we had found and presented to her and which she was taming." Percival's experience with the Roosevelt expedition convinced him that there was a living to be made as a professional hunter, while Roosevelt's book* African Game Trails *convinced the world that going on safari was a wonderful thing. The business of guided hunting boomed. Percival was in the right place at the right time, but he also had the skills and presence that let him manage camp staff, wild animals and (most difficult of all) wealthy and sometimes willful clients with equal success. In a trade that quickly became famous, sometimes infamous, for its characters, in his quiet way and without being a daredevil, a womanizer, a martinet, a braggart or a drinker, Percival stood out. His client roster eventually included royals, movie stars, famous naturalists and business tycoons. His peers thought equally highly of him and elected him president of EAPHA, the East African Professional Hunters Association, for 34 consecutive terms.*

*Percival was also one of the few professionals who was never mauled, gored, trampled, bitten, shot accidentally or otherwise seriously injured on the job. Luck surely played a role in this, but so did excellent judgment and a cool head as well as, occasionally, superb shooting ability.* John F. Kennedy Library

*East Africa, probably December 1933. Hemingway with the* faro, *the rhino, and his Springfield, already blooded on elk, deer and bear. Leicester Hemingway observed that his older brother "had come to have tremendous faith in [the .30-06's] accuracy and shocking power, even on the most dangerous sort of African game."* John F. Kennedy Library

holes. This somewhat reduces the carnage on a battlefield, but it is generally counterproductive on game, where the need is to kill as quickly as possible. Most hunting bullets are designed to penetrate the skin and then "mushroom"—expand to cut as many blood vessels and organs as possible. Ammunition companies began to make such bullets for the .30-06 very early on. Dozens, if not hundreds, eventually were developed, in weights ranging from 55 to 250 grains (⅛ to almost ⅝

ounces), which with different powder charges let the '06 handle everything from rodents to moose and bear. Theodore Roosevelt probably brought the first .30-06 to Africa, in 1909, and Stewart Edward White, the popular turn-of-the-century American novelist, the second one, in 1911. Before long it had proven itself there on all plains game (the various antelope and other hoofed species) and leopard and even, with reservations, on lion, Cape buffalo and rhino.

*More dangerous game fallen to the .30-06 on the first safari. One charging Cape buffalo finally died with its head in Hemingway's lap after being shot nearly a dozen times. The head of this buffalo hangs in the study at the Finca Vigía, Hemingway's home in San Francisco de Paula, just outside Havana, which is now a museum.*                                      John F. Kennedy Library

As a young boy, Ernest Hemingway—like so many American males —developed a serious case of hero worship for Theodore Roosevelt. He devoured Roosevelt's *African Game Trails* and surely noted its author's high praise for his custom-made Springfield .30-06 rifle. Hemingway would have one too. Every hunter dreams of Africa, its great gamefields, wide skies and elemental life; Ernest, a hunter since he could walk, would go to Africa also.

While the .30-06 cartridge soldiered on for 65 years with US forces, the Springfield rifle served from 1903 into the Second World War, since production of the new Garand rifle fell behind demand, and snipers used it in Korea and even Vietnam. (Many drill teams still carry Springfields in 21st Century Independence Day parades.) In official nomenclature, the Springfield was the "United States Rifle, Caliber .30, Model 1903." Its manually operated turnbolt action was so closely based on the design perfected in Germany a decade earlier that the American government had to pay Mauser about $1 million in royalties on the rifle, which would be used against the Mauser on the battlefields of both World Wars.

After a shot is fired, lifting the handle on the side of the action re-cocks the hammer and unlocks the breech bolt; pulling the bolt backward a few inches on its rails then extracts the empty cartridge shell from the firing chamber and kicks it away to the side. With the bolt slid back out of the way, a fresh round can rise, under spring pressure, from the magazine beneath. When the shooter shoves the bolt forward again, it scoops up the new cartridge and rams it into the chamber. Pushing the bolt handle down once more re-locks everything, ready for firing. The Springfield holds five rounds in its magazine and one in the chamber, and a practiced rifleman can empty a Springfield in well under a minute with accurate fire.

Until the advent of the modern assault rifle, secondhand-but-current army rifles were available to the American public. In 1905 the US Congress passed Public Law 149, which authorized the sale, at cost, of surplus military rifles, ammunition and certain equipment to accredited civilian shooting clubs. Two years earlier, Congress had established the National Board for the Promotion of Rifle Practice, to keep American citizens proficient in shooting in case of any future need to defend the country, either in uniformed service or as partisans fighting an invader. (Britain in 1859 and

America in 1871 had already formed civilian National Rifle Associations for almost the same purpose. Target shooting was a popular recreation at the turn of the 19th Century and both Queen Victoria and President Theodore Roosevelt took part—the latter much more avidly.)

While some of these sold surplus rifles were kept in original form and used for target shooting, many others went afield. Military rifles, however, generally are no more suitable for hunting than military ammunition, and by the time Hemingway acquired his, seemingly every gunsmith in America was converting ex-government Springfields, a process that became known as "sporterizing." This turned a roughly finished and heavy mass-produced tool into a rifle of some style and balance as well as high function. One of the best of the converters was a company called Griffin & Howe, which in 1930 became part of Abercrombie & Fitch, the hallowed New York sporting-goods store on Madison Avenue where Hemingway became a regular customer.

Seymour Griffin, a New York cabinet-maker, had bought a Springfield for himself in 1910. After reading, in *African Game Trails*, Roosevelt's comments about his Springfield ("the lightest and handiest of all my rifles") and noting that TR had had the rifle "stocked and sighted to suit myself," Seymour disassembled his own rifle, bought a length of walnut and shaped a handsome new stock for it. Friends then asked Griffin to modify their Springfields. This eventually led to a full-service gunsmithing and sales firm that

*Fall 1936. Hemingway is proud of this grizzly bear taken with his G&H Springfield at the Nordquist Ranch, in the Clark's Fork Valley of Wyoming. On the left, safari veteran Pauline Pfeiffer Hemingway has her 6.5mm Mannlicher-Schoenauer slung over her shoulder and son Patrick at her elbow; behind him are Tommy Shevlin, one of Hemingway's wealthy hunting and fishing pals, and Tommy's wife Lorraine.* John F. Kennedy Library

is still thriving. Griffin & Howe Springfields were deluxe goods and have become collectors' items. The record is unclear, but probably fewer than six hundred have been produced. Today, surplus Springfield rifles—which could in fact have been made by Remington, Smith Corona or the Rock Island Arsenal in addition to Springfield—are still available, and G&H will still convert one to order.

By chance, Ernest Hemingway and Milford Baker met in the elevator at Abercrombie & Fitch in the spring of 1929. As teenagers, they had driven ambulances together in Italy. Now, 11 years later, Hemingway was a young literary lion; Baker was knowledgeable about big-game hunting and rifles. Hemingway wanted Baker's advice; Baker wanted Hemingway's autograph on his books. As Hemingway was beginning to gear up for his first African safari, he launched an intense correspondence of more than a dozen letters (now at the Princeton University Library) with his old friend, writing that although he'd been shooting shotguns since he was 10 years old, he was a neophyte when it came to rifles. After some back-and-forth between them, Baker sought out Seymour Griffin—by this time, Griffin & Howe had become part of Abercrombie & Fitch—and in the course of an afternoon's conversation the two decided how to proceed with a rifle for Hemingway. Baker enlisted Hemingway in the National Rifle Association and then used his membership card to order, from the office of the Director of Civilian Marksmanship, a new, unfinished and unstocked National Match-quality Springfield barreled action selected by none other than Col. Townsend Whelen. Whelen was a blue-blooded soldier and hunter who became one of 20th Century America's most respected and influential firearms authorities. At the time, he was the director of research & development at the Springfield Armory. (For him to select a civilian customer's rifle was not unlike having Henry Ford pick out one's car.) The armory would ship the parts to Manhattan, where G&H would finish and equip the rifle to Baker's and Hemingway's specifications.

For proper stock dimensions, Hemingway wrote to Baker that he was six feet tall and weighed 190 pounds, with small hands for his size. He also provided the length of his neck and his right arm to the tip of his trigger finger, and enclosed a snapshot of himself so the stockmaker could see his overall proportions.

In 1930 G&H advertised that it could turn a sow's-ear army rifle into a silk-purse sporter for as little as $52.50. From a late-1920s G&H catalog: "In general the remodelling of a Springfield, as we do it, consists of fitting a new hand-made stock of imported walnut to fit the customer, polishing and re-blueing the barrel and action, matting the receiver ring, checkering the bolt handle, fitting a long matted ramp front sight base and special sights or telescopes of hunting type, and in general, converting a military musket to the latest and most approved type of hand-made bolt action sporting rifle."

During the Depression, surplus Springfields cost anywhere from $15 to $50, depending on grade and condition. Baker bought Hemingway's select barreled action for $30. Seymour Griffin charged $145 to build it into a best-grade rifle on a stock of Circassian walnut trimmed with a buffalo-horn forend tip and with the following fittings: an ivory-bead front sight mounted on a ramp and covered with a hood, paired with a Lyman No. 48 aperture-type rear sight; detachable sling swivels with a Whelen-style sling; and an engraved steel buttplate with a trapdoor covering a recess for spare cartridges and an extra sight. It received G&H Serial No. 956. In addition, G&H fitted one of its signature mounts (the early, single-lever type; $35) for a detachable telescopic sight and added a $2\frac{1}{4}$-power Zeiss Zielklein scope ($25). At Baker's recommendation, Hemingway also ordered a Heiser leather case for the rifle ($17.50) and a separate one for the scope ($4). The grand total came to $256.50—for a Springfield, Baker wrote, "built to the Queen's taste, which will fit you like a handmade Purdey."

Hemingway received his rifle in June 1930, in Key West, and was very pleased with it. He began to hunt with it that fall on his annual stay at the L-Bar-T Ranch in Wyoming. At first he enthused about how easy it was to attach and remove the scope from the rifle; in another letter he described watching a bear through it. However, Patrick Hemingway recalled that when his father first took the rifle elk hunting, "all he could see through the scope was a patch of hair." (This was a common problem with the primitive optics of early scopes, especially at fairly close range.) As well, Hemingway's eyeglasses made looking through a scope more difficult. He removed the sight and never used it again. In all the photographs of this rifle, taken on safaris 20 years apart as well as in the American West, it carries no scope. But the scope mount remained on the left side of the action.

*Youth and experience; Idaho, October 1946. Patrick Hemingway at 18 with a superb mule deer that fell to one well-placed bullet from the Springfield loaned by Papa. (Patrick's first big-game animal was probably a whitetail deer taken on Gardiners Island, NY, in 1943.) At 21, Patrick moved to East Africa, where for 25 years he was a professional hunter, a forestry officer and an instructor of game wardens and professional hunters. The Sun Valley Resort's chief guide, Taylor Williams, was a close friend of the Hemingway family.*

Lloyd Arnold/John F. Kennedy Library

Off-the-rack .30-06 bolt-action sporting rifles from Winchester and Remington cost about $53 in 1930, while a commercial Mauser .30-06 from Germany—readily available, if not common, in the US at the time—was $110 (the equivalent of about $1,400 in 2010). A high-grade .30-caliber bolt-action by premier English makers such as Holland & Holland and Purdey retailed for about £35 in 1934, equivalent then to $175. That was in London, though, and importers doubled the UK price in the US. By 1940 inflation in Britain and a weakening of the American dollar had tripled the price of such rifles in the US. Hemingway's Griffin & Howe Springfield looked more and more like a bargain as time went on.

In the section of *Green Hills of Africa* that starts this chapter, before Hemingway shot at the *faro*, the rhino, with his Springfield, he opened the bolt to make sure the rifle was loaded with "solids," specifically the 220-grain non-expanding bullets he favored for big game. He never identified it as a white or a black rhino, but no matter—an African rhinoceros can mass three tons and stand six feet at the shoulders, and its hide is nearly two inches thick in places. Driving a bullet through that much armor and tissue to a vital organ takes accuracy and a degree of luck, or great power, or all three. Hemingway knew that a soft-nose bullet would likely deform and stop before doing much damage to such a massive animal, so he opted for one that would stay in one piece and go deep. Or so he hoped. Today a .30-06 is considered nowhere near "enough gun" for rhino, and even in 1933 it was well on the light side of such proven heavy bolt-action calibers as the .375 Holland & Holland Magnum and the .416 Rigby, which were available

by 1912 (and which Milford Baker had recommended to Hemingway in their 1930 letters). Both, however, were English cartridges developed for Africa and India and uncommon in America. (By the 1950s, Kenya had set minimum calibers for safari clients to use on dangerous game. The .30-06 falls far short.)

Hemingway had by 1933 taken deer, elk, mountain sheep and several grizzly bears with his '06 and had become a devout believer in its accuracy and lethality. In Africa, he knew that in most circumstances he could shoot his light rifle because his professional hunter was backing him up with heavy artillery—Philip Percival then carried a double-barreled .450 No. 2 Nitro Express. Decades later, Mary wrote that her husband "killed buffalo, three lions, and 27 other animals" with his Springfield on his first safari.[2] Papa told her they were all one-shot kills, which is so unlikely as to be virtually impossible.

To a hunter accustomed to elk and deer as big game, a 220-grain bullet may have seemed to be an adequate step up (from the usual North American bullets of 140 to 180 grains) for *big* big game. However, at the time the normal bullet for the .375 H&H, the smallest of the accepted dangerous-game calibers, weighed 300 grains and the .416's was 400 or 410 grains. And note that when a charge by the wounded rhino seemed imminent, "Pop" (Percival) cautioned Hemingway to "take the big gun"—a double-barreled .470 Nitro Express, a far more effective short-range stopper than any .30-caliber. (Hemingway's double rifles are discussed elsewhere.)

That a .30-06 bullet, even a 220-grain solid, caused a fatal wound on a thick-skinned, massively boned animal at "all of three hundred" yards is surprising enough; that Hemingway would even shoot at a rhino at that distance verges on lunacy. Was this factual? His ego at play? Inability to gauge distance (not unusual even for experienced hunters)? Literary invention?

Today, when virtually everyone shoots with telescopic sights, we tend to forget how accurate an expert could be without them. To qualify for Col. Hiram Berdan's Union Army sharpshooter regiments during America's War Between the States, a man had to be able to put 10 consecutive shots "from the shoulder"—i.e., not from a fixed support—into a 10-inch circle at 200 yards with open, so-called "iron" sights. (Gunsights with glass lenses date back to the 17th Century.) Given the aperture, or ring-type, rear sight on Hemingway's Springfield, he should have been able to hit an animal the size of an automobile fairly easily at 300 yards; nevertheless, even a rhinoceros is half-obscured by the front sight bead at that range and precise bullet placement is not possible. In this case the odds against immobilizing, not to say killing, the animal are high. By the time the hunters reached the spot, the result could be a lightly wounded rhino, bad-tempered and looking for trouble—or a flat-out miss. By any standard, this sort of shooting is irresponsible, even with a more powerful rifle. Hemingway

*Same Springfield, second safari, August 1953 into January '54. The rifle has now been Hemingway's for 24 years. Lloyd Arnold called it "the patinaed, mellow-with-use gun—the one that Ernest really cared for, personally, above others." The scope is long gone, but its single-lever G&H mount, on the left side of the receiver, remains.*

John F. Kennedy Library

was a very capable game shot when he was in his 30s, but at that range and with such a light caliber—especially without the magnification and precision of a scope—this qualifies as the sort of luck that lets drunks walk away from horrific car wrecks without a scratch.

Twenty years later, however, in *Rogue* Magazine, Denis Zaphiro wrote that he watched

Papa kill a gazelle at 400 yards with this same .30-06—after spurning Zaphiro's offer of a rifle with a scope. "Take that away, boy," he said to Zaphiro; "those are for nuns and virgins."

Dangerous game is normally "engaged" at less than a hundred yards. Close range allows much more accurate shooting and lets the shooter see where the animal goes, if it isn't accommodating enough to fall down on the spot. (Two decades earlier, Theodore Roosevelt had earned a dodgy reputation for opening fire on animals, even dangerous ones, at long range, and his eyesight was worse than Hemingway's.)

Then: "He had that damned Springfield cocked," wrote Hemingway. "The cocked gun behind my back made me black angry."

He emphatically did not want an inexperienced man behind him in a dicey spot with a rifle that was ready to fire. (Even if the safety catch had been on—Hemingway doesn't mention it—safeties have a way of mysteriously switching themselves to "off" in such situations.) However, Hemingway himself is to blame. It happened just as he described it: "Droopy was running and I re-loaded and ran off after him." The rifle cocked when he opened the bolt and worked the action to re-load—and, clearly in a hurry, he did not de-cock it before swapping with Droopy for the "big gun." De-cocking a bolt action is a deliberate two-handed movement that is almost impossible to do while running. In the heat of the moment Hemingway unthinkingly handed his cocked Springfield to someone unfamiliar with firearms. Accidents with

guns are more common on safari than being mauled by animals; that an experienced hunter like Hemingway could make such a mistake shows why.

(Pauline recorded in her journal an incident when Ernest's rifle—she doesn't specify which one, the .30-06 or the .470—fell off the safari car roof and, supposedly safe, discharged next to her husband when it hit the ground. She thought he'd been killed.)

The hunting climax of *Under Kilimanjaro* and *True at First Light*, the books about the second safari, is Mary Hemingway's black-maned lion: After much fruitless tracking and frustration, the animal was found out in the open in good, though fast-fading, shooting light. "G.C." (Gin-Crazed; Hemingway's nickname for the oh-so-British Zaphiro) stalked very close with Mary while Hemingway took up a flanking position farther away. Mary's first bullet hit the lion in the foot. It bolted. Everyone opened fire. The lion had been only lightly wounded, so the overriding concern was to anchor it before it could get out of sight. Instead of running in the direction Hemingway was blocking, the lion turned and went the other way, toward the forest. Tactically, a good choice—go for cover and then make a stand, as lions often do.

However, as the story unfolds, G.C. is shooting his heavy, short-range double rifle and misses—the range is opening up and too great. Hemingway fires his Springfield and sees dirt spurt up three times where *he* missed. On his fourth shot the lion, now "beginning to look small in the sights," suddenly goes down. Hemingway's bullet has broken its spine at a distance so great that he and G.C. later measured it with the odometer of the Land Rover and then promised each other that they would "never, never tell anybody how long a shot it was, drunk or sober with shits or decent people." [3]

Every shooter eventually makes some impossibly lucky shots, usually when they don't know better than to try or in situations where a hail-Mary effort is justifiable. And some shooters are novelists. Mary's own account of this episode[2] is quite different and far less dramatic, and the fatal shot, at close range, is from Zaphiro's rifle. A brilliant storyteller, Hemingway had made the event "truer than if it had really happened."

*The mid-'50s safari. Mayito Menocal, Hemingway's Cuban friend, killed the leopard, but time was running out and* Look *needed the photo. After posing with his .30-06, Papa promised Mary that he would soon shoot a* chui *of his own, to salve her conscience about "phony" pictures. And he did, three months later.*

Earl Theisen/John F. Kennedy Library

Two years after his death, Papa's treasured .30-06, G&H Serial No. 956, was one of the two rifles and two shotguns that Mary Hemingway consigned to Abercrombie & Fitch to be sold. The A&F ledger indicates that its selling price would be $150. However, Mary withdrew the Springfield two weeks later and then kept it at the house in Ketchum until she finally gave it to Patrick. He hunted with it and once shot a moose with it. It was stolen from his home in Montana in the late 1970s. Collectors periodically think they have found the missing rifle, one of the sporting world's grails, but the claims have never stood up. At the time, the police concluded that it may have been part of a haul of weapons destined for the Irish Republican Army.

# MANNLICHER-SCHOENAUER RIFLES

*Antelope hunting got two marvellous bucks . . . both running, dead, one-shot mannlicher.*

—to Arnold Gingrich, 16 September, 1936,
while Hemingway was at the Nordquist Ranch, Wyoming

The bolt-action rifle made its commercial debut in 1841, when the Dreyse *Zündnadelgewehr*, or "needle-fire," single-shot entered military service in Prussia. With it came the one-piece cartridge—ammunition that combined a percussion cap, propellant and projectile in a self-contained unit that was fed into the gun barrel from its breech (as opposed to laboriously shoving in powder, wadding and ball from the muzzle end, as had been done for five or six centuries). The Dreyse was followed by the Chassepot rifle—also named for its designer—which was adopted in 1866 by the army of France. Just four years later the Chassepot went into combat in the Franco-Prussian War, where it greatly outperformed the Dreyse.

Both these rifles, however, fired low-power cartridges contained in fragile paper tubes, while more robust ammunition in foil or drawn-brass cases was appearing in England and the United States—the next critical advancement in firearms development.

Having won his war with France in 1871, Kaiser Wilhelm I handed over thousands of captured Chassepot rifles to a number of gunmakers—including Paul and Wilhelm Mauser in the town of Oberndorf, in southeastern Germany—for conversion to Germany's brand-new 11x60mm blackpowder metallic cartridge. Assisted by an American named Samuel Norris, of what would become Remington Arms, the Mauser brothers' Model 1871 rifle was developed in conjunction with this round. This was the first of untold millions of bolt-action repeating rifles to bear the Mauser name.

France, meanwhile, advanced to a rifle called the Gras, an evolution of the Chassepot, and its cartridge, which also now had a brass case. Switzerland, Italy, Austria, the US and Britain were involved in this game of battle-rifle one-upmanship as well, along with Germany and France.

On the heels of the move from paper to brass cartridge cases came the momentous step from black to smokeless gunpowder, which burned not only much more cleanly but also took up less space and generated more energy. Together, these advancements drove a steady progression to ever-smaller calibers—that is, smaller-diameter bullets that flew faster and more accurately. A single-shot muzzleloading musket of the American Revolution or the Napoleonic Wars weighed more than 10 pounds and typically fired about a .75-caliber (nearly three-quarter-inch) ounce-and-a-quarter lead ball at about 1,000 feet per second; it belched a cloud of whitish smoke and at a hundred yards was likely to miss a target the size of a man's head, if not the man himself. A century later, the 6.5x54mm Mannlicher cartridge,

By 1881 the Remington Arms Company had a bolt-action repeating rifle that fired metallic blackpowder cartridges fed from a detachable box magazine, designed by James Paris Lee, but the US Army officially ignored such advancements until it began to test magazine rifles in 1890. Yet as late as the Spanish-American War of 1898, many American troops were still armed with single-shot breechloading muskets. Thanks to the influence of their colonel, Theodore Roosevelt, the 1st US Volunteer Cavalry Regiment (aka the Rough Rid-

*Mannlicher-Schoenauer Model 1903 Serial No. 18040—Hemingway's second (or third?) 6.5x54mm carbine, which he and Lloyd Arnold won in a raffle in Sun Valley in 1941. Pulling the rear trigger "set" the forward trigger—reduced its let-off weight from a few pounds to a few ounces, for better accuracy on a precise shot. On his first Mannlicher, bought in 1930, Hemingway had Griffin & Howe replace the European triggers with an American-style single trigger.*

Bonhams & Butterfields

developed in Austria, launched a streamlined bullet a quarter-inch in diameter and weighing a third of an ounce at 2,300 feet per second—with no vision-obscuring smoke or barrel-fouling residue. Its rifle, a magazine-fed repeater, weighed less than seven pounds and at a hundred yards was accurate to within an inch or so. The musket ball lost all effectiveness by 200 yards; the swift and aerodynamic 6.5mm bullet could reliably hit an enemy soldier at 500 yards plus.

ers) had Norwegian-designed Krag-Jørgensen bolt-action repeaters, but they suffered badly in their charge up San Juan Hill at the hands of Spanish troops carrying Mausers. The Krag was speedily replaced by the 1903 Springfield rifle. If America came late to the bolt-action party, at least the Springfield, and the .30 Govt. cartridge developed for it, took advantage of the pioneering work that had gone on in Europe.

All these advancements were driven entirely by nationalistic desires for the most effective military weapons, but hunters and target shooters profited as well.

(It is mildly fascinating that Theodore Roosevelt took a Springfield .30-06—which came about partly because of his troops' disastrous experience against Mausers in Cuba—to East Africa; and that his fervent admirer Ernest Hemingway would follow him to Kenya with the same rifle, a near clone of the Mauser, and then settle in Cuba.)

Ernest Hemingway chose a Springfield as the basis for his first high-powered hunting rifle in early 1930, but by July of that year he was already writing to Milford Baker that, at nine pounds, his .30-06 was too heavy to carry up and down the mountains and he wanted something lighter. As their correspondence makes clear, he decided on, and ordered from Griffin & Howe, a Mannlicher-Schoenauer Model 1903, caliber 6.5x54mm—slightly less powerful than his Springfield but shorter in length and three pounds lighter.

Apparently this was not Ernest's first encounter with a Mannlicher. Leicester Hemingway recalled that his big brother (nearly 16 years older) returned from the ambulance corps in Italy in 1918 with war souvenirs that included a military Mannlicher with a straight-pull bolt:

"'That's a sniper's rifle,' he told me. 'I killed the sniper who was using it to pick off our troops from up in a tree.'" [1]

Ferdinand Mannlicher was a prolific and far-sighted German-born gun designer who in 1877 joined Steyr, Austria's industrial arms manufacturer, and three years later had created his first bolt-action rifle. This underwent steady modifications, including a detachable box-style magazine and a clip-fed loading system, and then the transition from black to smokeless powder, with its different combustion characteristics. In 1886 a gunmaker named Otto Schönauer joined Steyr, and he and Mannlicher collaborated to create a rifle that was ultimately unsuccessful as a military weapon but is still revered today for hunting. Mannlicher was ennobled for his work in 1887, becoming Ferdinand Ritter (knight) von Mannlicher. Herr Schönauer became Technical Director of Steyr; his name has ever since been Anglicized to "Schoenauer."

Their famous Mannlicher-Schoenauer rifle was a combination of the former's turn-bolt action and the latter's unique magazine. It appeared in 1899, was displayed at the Paris Exposition in 1900, and went into commercial production as the Model 1903. Fond as he was of his Griffin & Howe Springfield, Hemingway apparently only ever had one .30-06, but he may have had as many as four Mannlicher-Schoenauers, and he used them in Africa, Cuba, Wyoming and Idaho and perhaps elsewhere.

In nearly all bolt-action rifles, including Mannlicher's first models, the reserve cartridges lie one atop the other in the magazine, the well beneath the bolt. The Mannlicher-Schoenauer has a rotary magazine; five rounds fit neatly into a horizontal spool that turns to feed each cartridge upward, where the bolt can

*East Africa, late 1933 or early '34. Pauline Pfeiffer Hemingway with an impressively horned Thompson's gazelle, evidently taken with this Model 1903 Mannlicher-Schoenauer 6.5x54mm carbine. The bracket of what looks like a Griffin & Howe single-lever detachable scope mount is visible on the left side of the action, just above her thumb; had this rifle been bought in Paris en route to Kenya, it likely would have had an offset European claw- or rail-type scope mount instead. (Because of their split rear receiver rings, Mannlichers won't accept conventional scope mounts.) This is presumably also the rifle Pauline is holding in the 1936 photo on page 75. There seems to be no band around the barrel where the sling is attached.* John F. Kennedy Library

*Idaho, fall 1940. Hemingway poses for a publicity photo with cleaning rod in hand and looking down the bore of a battered Mannlicher-Schoenauer carbine. This is not the "raffle rifle" (No. 18040, which was acquired a year later) but probably the one he bought from Griffin & Howe in 1930, which had a single trigger installed. Note the scope-mount bracket beyond the ejection port and the barrel band at the sling loop. It may be the rifle now in the Finca Vigía in Cuba—but is it the rifle that Pauline used in Kenya?* Lloyd Arnold/ John F. Kennedy Library

grab it and slide it forward into the breech. It's a thing of mechanical beauty but too complex for a military weapon, which should be inexpensive to manufacture as well as dirt- and idiot-proof. (Nevertheless, the Model 1903 served in the Greek army through World War II.) The rotary magazine also restricts the size of the cartridge that can be accommodated, another reason the Mauser-type bolt-action eventually prevailed among big-game hunters who didn't want or couldn't afford heavy double rifles.

The box magazine of a Mauser can be made roomy enough to stack even the cigar-thick .505 Gibbs cartridges; but to fit them into a round carousel would have given the Mannlicher-Schoenauer a pregnant belly. This wasn't a problem with slender cartridges such as the 6.5x54mm round that helped make the high-quality, svelte, beautiful-handling Mannlicher the famous "gentleman's rifle." The British called it by its inch-equivalent bore diameter, .256, and ignored the 54mm designation, which is the length of the cartridge case. Like the Nitro Express calibers for big game, the .256/6.5 Mannlicher was a technological breakthrough, one that suddenly changed the rules on stalking medium-size game at the turn of the 19th Century. Its performance is still respectable today; a century ago it was fantastic. Since it added 200 yards or more to the range at which a stag or chamois could be killed, European and British sportsmen of the day quickly adapted it to hunting and then, inevitably, took it to Africa.

However, the Springfield's .30-06 cartridge eventually became far more popular than the .256 because its greater size made it adaptable

*Kenya, late 1953 or early '54. Mary shooting the Rothschild/Percival Mannlicher-Schoenauer rifle. She is just coming out of the recoil. The gun has left her shoulder, her eyes are closed and she's slumped slightly backward, laughing, with the stub of a cigarette still in her right hand. (No wonder she was an erratic shot.) Her nails are manicured and painted. Denis Zaphiro is enthusiastic, looking downrange at the target, exclaiming and clapping in support. Two friends clearly enjoying a moment.*

*Zaphiro, a former* bimbashi—*major—in the Sudan Defence Force, was the game warden in the Kajiado District, where the Hemingways were camped. His father, Fotios (aka Philip) Zaphiro, stands out in East African history: a Greek born in Cairo who became Her Majesty's Consul at Mega, in southern Abyssinia, and was responsible for setting the present international border and who single-handedly administered a large part of northern Kenya on behalf of the Crown in the days before there was any formal government there. Denis was a proper British public-school type, quiet but with a dry, wry sense of humor, good manners, and evident empathy and patience. He was, of necessity, a crack shot and cool under pressure—traits that Hemingway valued highly. He grew close to both Ernest and Mary and in 1957 spent nearly four months as their house guest in Cuba and the US. Zaphiro became one of the first of Kenya's flying wardens (Hemingway may have given him, in addition to his Woodsman pistol, an airplane!) and retired from the Game Department in the 1970s as a highly regarded veteran. Mary, when she died in 1986, left him $5,000—although his name appears in her will as "Dennis Shapiro." Under Hemingway's tongue-in-cheek nickname "G.C."—for Gin-Crazed, from the British fondness for gin in general and gin & tonics in the tropics—Zaphiro became a major character in* Under Kilimanjaro *and* True at First Light.

Earl Theisen/John F. Kennedy Library

*Kenya, late 1953 or early '54. Hemingway holds the customized Mannlicher-Schoenauer rifle (note the longer barrel and the shorter stock forend) that Mary had borrowed from Philip Percival, their professional hunter. The take-down joint, an inch and a half above the magazine floorplate, is clearly visible.*

Earl Theisen/John F. Kennedy Library

As Hemingway learned on his first safari, by 1933 the .256 had made many friends in Africa. Professionals saw no reason to shoot big, expensive, hard-recoiling Express or Magnum cartridges when lighter, cheaper ammunition would do. Typically expert shots, many of them used the .256 for everything from camp meat to, occasionally, elephants—when they were on their own and could control the situation. (They usually had their tracker/gunbearer along with a heavy back-up rifle in case something went wrong.) The solid, non-expanding version of the .256's 160-grain bullet, small in cross-section and disproportionately long, could reach the vitals of even a big animal, provided the shooter placed it precisely. But the Mannlicher was far too light for protecting clients, who couldn't be counted on to kill dangerous game with one shot or who spooked the animals into wariness.

to more kinds of game and shooting. By 1924 Mannlicher-Schoenauer rifles were also available in .30-06 as well as half a dozen other calibers.

*P*hilip, who swears by the .450 No. 2 as the only, or at least the lightest, stopper for a man to use on animals that will "come," killed all his own lions with a .256 Mannlicher when he had only his own life to look after. [2]

A light, easy-recoiling, accurate rifle with a jewel-like bolt mechanism was also ideal for women, and two Hemingway wives on three safaris used a Mannlicher, although not the same one. One of Hemingway's famous fictional characters used one as well, to shocking effect: Margaret Macomber ended "The Short Happy Life of Francis Macomber" with one shot from a 6.5mm Mannlicher.

Second wife Pauline's rifle, on the first safari, was a compact Schoenauer carbine, with its distinctive short barrel and full-length European stock. Leicester wrote that his brother bought it in Paris, en route to East Africa on 1933. At the time, the retail price in the US of a Mannlicher-Schoenauer was an even $100, double the cost of a comparable American rifle; in Europe it was surely far less expensive, especially for the strong

*Kenya, late 1953 or early '54. Mary beams proudly over an excellent lesser kudu bull while Papa looks on in apparent resignation. A gunbearer holds the take-down Mannlicher-Schoenauer with which she probably shot the animal.*

Earl Theisen/John F. Kennedy Library

dollar. But would the Hemingways leave behind the Mannlicher-Schoenauer that Ernest had bought from Griffin & Howe three years earlier, only to buy an identical one in France? Would such a rifle also have the G&H-style scope mount that appears in the photo of Pauline with her African Tommy? Leicester's gun savvy is sometimes questionable—he wrote [1] that Ernest killed himself with a "silver-inlaid 12-gauge double-barreled Richardson shotgun" (there is no such thing)—and in the many appearances of a Mannlicher-Schoenauer throughout the 1930s in narratives, letters and memoirs by or about Hemingway, the mention is always of one gun, with no indication that the family had two of them at the time. Yet Pauline's safari carbine appears to be different from the one Ernest is holding in the 1940 Idaho publicity photo—it has no barrel band.

There is a Mannlicher-Schoenauer carbine at the Finca Vigía, the Hemingway home outside Havana that is now Cuba's most famous museum, but requests for its serial number have so far gone unanswered. If that number matches one from Griffin & Howe's inventory records of the late 1920s, the provenance of that rifle will be established—but we still won't know definitively whether Ernest and Pauline did buy a second Mannlicher in Paris in November 1933 and, perhaps, left it behind in Africa when they departed in February 1934.

In any event, throughout the 1930s a Mannlicher-Schoenauer carbine spent much time in an oil-soaked sheepskin case aboard *Pilar*, Ernest's boat, where it was used to fend off sharks homing in on gamefish brought to the transom. In May 1936 Hemingway wrote, in *Esquire*, of an encounter with a whale that sent his Cuban friends into ecstasy. ("A whale is worth a fortune in La Habana!") They would try to harpoon it and then put "solids from the Mannlicher" into it and, finally, inflate the carcass with the air-mattress pump and tow it back to harbor. Not surprisingly, the whale failed to cooperate.

Hemingway arrived at the Sun Valley Resort in Idaho—in a dusty black Buick convertible with Martha Gellhorn, his new wife-to-be—for the first time in September 1939. Much later, Lloyd Arnold recalled the occasion, and being shown Hemingway's guns: "So out they all came: the lovely old Griffin &

Howe Springfield of *Green Hills of Africa*; Pauline's little 6.5 Mannlicher, or that which literally done in poor Francis Macomber; a couple of .22 plinking rifles; and two shotguns made to order for our country." [3] It seems a Mannlicher was not part of any divorce settlement with Pauline.

Hemingway acquired a second (third?) Mannlicher in Idaho in 1941. An employee in the Sun Valley Inn kitchen was moving on, Arnold wrote, and had "a little 6.5 caliber Mannlicher-Schoenauer carbine—identical to [Hemingway's] except for double-set hair triggers" that he wanted to get rid of. Instead of selling it directly, the cook raffled it off, with tickets going for a dollar apiece. At dinner one evening, "fairly well taken in the juice of the grape," [3] Ernest and Lloyd pooled their pocket money and bought half a dozen tickets, and together won the rifle. Upon his annual return to Sun Valley from the Finca Vigía, in September 1947, Hemingway turned it over to Lloyd Arnold for keeps, remarking that he had had to resort to some sort of ruse to get his favorite guns out of Cuba and adding that the Mannlicher now had a "big fish-eating shark" to its credit.

Some time after Lloyd's death, in 1970, his wife Tillie sold this rifle, which we now know was a Model 1903, Serial No. 18040. The new owner in turn consigned it to Butterfield & Butterfield, the San Francisco auction house that is now part of Bonham's, where it fetched $6,325 in a sale on 17 November 1997. (Tillie Arnold died in California at the

*Mannlicher-Schoenauer Model 1952 Serial No. 14482, caliber 6.5x54mm, bought from Abercrombie & Fitch in 1954. Mary Hemingway took this on safari in 1963 and willed it to her friend Bud Purdy after her death, in 1986. Her initials are engraved on the stock oval and the luggage tag on its leather case reads: Mrs. Ernest Hemingway, 27 East 56th St, New York, N.Y. 10021.* Andy Kent

age of 99 in January 2005. In July of that year, she and Lloyd, who had been buried in Iowa, were re-interred in a plot adjacent to Mary and Ernest Hemingway in Ketchum, Idaho. Other members of Hemingway's "tribe" lie nearby as well.)

Ernest and Martha Gellhorn divorced at the end of 1945. On 14 March 1946, in Havana, Ernest was re-married for the last time, to Mary Welsh. Like Pauline 20 years earlier, Mary Welsh Hemingway also carried a 6.5mm Mannlicher-Schoenauer on safari, but a different one yet—a rifle (not a carbine) with a conventional three-quarter-length stock and a longer barrel, as well as a take-down mechanism of the kind offered by gunmakers such as Westley Richards in England, not by Steyr. The barrel and forend could be separated quickly from the action and buttstock for more convenient travel or storage. Mary shot many, maybe all, of her trophies with it, but not easily. Years later, she wrote about her performance on safari

*The Double R Ranch, Picabo, Idaho, July 2008. Legendary rancher Bud Purdy, age 90, with Mannlicher-Schoenauer No. 14482. Behind him flows Silver Creek.* Roger Sanger

with Ernest: "I had shot badly and missed animals time after time, I decided, because privately I couldn't bear to kill them." There was a more practical problem also, namely that the rifle was, as her husband noted afterward, too "long-stocked." [4]

*I did not think about Miss Mary except about her height, which was five feet two inches, in relation to tall grass and bush and that, no matter how cold the morning was, she must not wear too much clothing as the stock on the 6.5 Mannlicher was too long for her if her shoulder was padded and she might let the rifle off as she raised it to shoot.* [5]

Since Hemingway already owned at least one Mannlicher carbine—or two, including the one he'd handed over to Lloyd Arnold; or three, if Pauline's gun was a different one yet and was still available—why not bring one of them to Africa for Mary? For whatever reason, Hemingway did not. Instead, the rifle Mary carried was on loan from Philip Percival, "Pop," who had been given it by a client, a member of the Rothschild family, before the Second World War.

*Mary was holding her rifle straight up and I had a fine view of the new-wiped dark barrel and the Scotch tape that held her rear-sight leaves down, of the back of her head and her disreputable hat.*[5]

Mary's rifle had British-style open sights—a bead on a ramp at the muzzle and a shallow V-type rear sight. The rear sight had two leaves, one behind the other and the second one hinged to lie flat, out of the way when not needed. Each leaf was marked for a certain distance—100 and 300 yards, perhaps—and to prevent the wrong leaf

from being used accidentally, the other one was taped down. Scotch Tape, by the way, was already 20 years old by the time of this safari. (We know Hemingway didn't like telescopic sights, but Mary's shooting surely would have been improved by one.)

Finally, back home again in Cuba, Papa promised Mary "a beautiful gun that really fits and cannot miss." [4] In August 1956 he bought another 6.5x54 Mannlicher-Schoenauer carbine from Abercrombie & Fitch, a Model 1952 this time, Serial No. 14482. The price was $198. Mary apparently had no immediate use for it, as the Hemingways did not take delivery of it until October 1958.

Ernest died on 2 July 1961. In May 1962, Mary traveled from Idaho "with my beautiful Mannlicher-Schoenauer 6.5 rifle and my Winchester Model-21, 20-gauge shotgun, old outdoors companions" [4] to join her friend Clara Spiegel on safari with Patrick Hemingway in Tanganyika. A photograph from this trip shows Mary posing with a dead leopard by the light of a camp lantern; she is holding a rifle with a scope—Clara's Winchester Model 70. Mary may have borrowed it for a low-light shot on a dangerous cat precisely because it had a scope. She felt no compunction in shooting the leopard; it was blamed for killing and eating a child from a nearby village.

The 11th directive in the Last Will and Testament of Mary Hemingway, executed after her death on 26 November 1986, was that her Mannlicher-Schoenauer, No. 14482, was to go to her old friend Bud Purdy, of Picabo, Idaho. It remains in his possession today.

# THE .577 NITRO EXPRESS (& OTHER DOUBLE RIFLES)

*I wondered . . . if there should be anything wrong with Sen. Joe McCarthy (Republican) of Wisconsin which a .577 solid would not cure.*

"The Christmas Gift," *Look*, April 20/May 4, 1954

*Then* I took the .577 and held low on the point of his fore-shoulder. Shooting prone I knew the .577 could break my shoulder but probably only the collarbone. But it would break the old bull's shoulder. With the safety on I squeezed on him. [1]

Ernest Hemingway's double-barreled .577-caliber rifle was an English Nitro Express, not the obsolete 19th Century blackpowder version of the same cartridge. Nearly six-tenths of an inch in diameter, the .577 NE's standard bullet weighs almost an ounce and three-quarters and, fired at a velocity of some 2,050 feet per second, generates a devastating 6,600-plus foot-pounds of striking energy. The

.577 is a stopper indeed and, in the words of many a bruised Brit, a "right bastard to shoot." At the wooden end, a .577 NE produces more than a hundred foot-pounds of recoil, leading some wags to say that it kicked the shooter out of the path of a charging animal.

Leonard Lyons in his *New York Post* column of 26 June 1953 wrote that he had accompanied Hemingway to the basement shooting range at Abercrombie & Fitch, where Papa wanted to test-fire some old .577 cartridges. Papa induced Lyons to shoot too: ". . . the recoil hurled me back against the back of the cement booth and the gun fell from my

*Westley Richards No. 17425 was built for Stephen Henry Christy, of Plaish Hall, Church Stretton, Shropshire, England, as "a double hammerless detachable-lock, single-trigger full-load .577 rifle." It was completed in October 1913. Forty years later, Ernest Hemingway carried it on safari in East Africa—after it had rubbed shoulders with the likes of Bror Blixen and Beryl Markham.*

Curry Mansion Inn, Key West

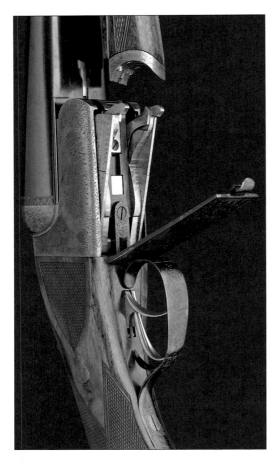

*"The construction of the locks is excellent and simple to a degree, so that should anything go wrong with the mechanism in the bush, where you cannot take a taxi to your gunmaker, there is no difficulty in instantly detaching a lock by hand and replacing it with a duplicate." Westley Richards calls this its hand-detachable-lock action; the shooting world simply refers to it as the Westley droplock. Many professional big-game hunters regard it as the pinnacle of double-rifle design and construction.*

Andrew Orr/Holt's Auctioneers

hand. 'You OK?' the salesman asked. Only a wrenched shoulder. 'Lucky,' he said. 'They usually break a collar-bone.'"

Touching off a .577 while lying on the ground, as Hemingway knew, is asking for trouble, since the body can't absorb some of the awful recoil by flexing backward. But Hemingway never intended to shoot from the prone position; he was going through the motions just to show that he could have killed the buffalo. Apparently he did kill at least one lion with his .577, as well as a rhino that had been wounded prior and perhaps the buffalo shown here. He never shot an elephant, on either safari. And, fortunately, he never got to shoot his .577 at a German U-boat (below).

Even among so-called elephant rifles, the .577 Nitro Express is very nearly overkill, but it was favored by a few professionals, especially when they were facing aggressive animals in thick cover and wanted overwhelming shocking power and penetration. Jim Sutherland, a famous ivory hunter, was a fan; in his 1912 book *The Adventures of an Elephant Hunter*, he noted: "After experimenting with and using all kinds of rifles, I find the most effective to be the double .577 with a 750 grain bullet and a charge in Axite powder equivalent to a hundred grains of cordite. The heavier double-barrelled .600 bore rifle, with a bullet weighing 900 grains, lacks the penetration of the .577, while its weight (16 lbs. against 13 lbs. of the latter) renders it a much more awkward weapon to handle. I think the superiority of the .577 over the .450 and .500 rifles will be evident when I state that I have lost elephants

*The second safari. Hemingway with a fine, thick-bossed—if oddly portly—Cape buffalo and his Westley Richards double .577 Nitro Express rifle. In another photo of this buffalo, Hemingway is holding his Springfield .30-06.*                           John F. Kennedy Library

with these last two rifles, while I have bagged others with identically the same shots from a .577."

Hemingway provides no clues about the provenance of his .577, but photographs and Mary's and Patrick's recollections identify it as a Westley Richards. By its very nature, such an unusual and single-purpose weapon invariably has a tale to tell, but the history of this one is remarkable even by the standards of Hemingway's fantastic life.

Traditional London firms such as Purdey and Holland & Holland have for nearly 200 years built small numbers of costly, bespoke sporting guns and rifles for the carriage trade. The city of Birmingham, a hundred miles to the north in England's industrial

Midlands, was home to the gunmakers who manufactured the untold quantities of more plebian firearms that British troops and traders carried around the world during the heyday of the Empire. Several of these companies were also capable of building guns that rivaled London's best, and Westley Richards was and still is one of them.

William Westley Richards established the firm in 1812 and two years later opened a retail shop in Mayfair, the toney part of London that was the natural habitat of many of Britain's aristocratic sportsmen. The company became famous not just for quality, but also for gunmaking advancements. In 1875 Westley Richards employees William Anson and John Deeley invented the so-called boxlock, an elegantly simple cocking and firing mechanism for double-barreled guns that remains the strongest, most successful and widely used to this today. During the next eight decades, Westley's earned more than 75 patents, medals and royal warrants as gunmakers to Indian and Far Eastern maharajahs, sultans, nawabs and emperors as well as British, Continental and Middle Eastern crowned heads, including His Majesty King Edward VII.

Leslie B. Taylor, who became Westley Richards' managing director in 1890, devised a way to make Anson & Deeley's lockwork easily removable (and thus replaceable) through a hinged floorplate in the bottom of the gun. To an almost foolproof system, this added another level of surety, a belt-and-suspenders approach that greatly impressed big-game hunters. Jim Sutherland: "The double-barrelled

.577 which I have used for several years and found admirable in every detail was built for me by Westley Richards & Co., of Bond Street. The construction of the locks is excellent and simple to a degree, so that should anything go wrong with the mechanism in the bush, where you cannot take a taxi to your gunmaker, there is no difficulty in instantly detaching a lock by hand and replacing it with a duplicate."

Westley's calls this its hand-detachable lock action; the shooting world simply refers to it as the Westley droplock. Many professionals regard it as the pinnacle of double-rifle design and construction.

Leslie Taylor is also credited with developing the company's successful single trigger. The challenge was to devise one trigger that could reliably fire both barrels, one after the other, with no risk of the recoil of the first, however severe, jarring off the second one by accident, directly or indirectly. (Many double-barreled shotguns and rifles sidestep this problem by having two triggers—a separate one for each lock and barrel.) Sutherland again: "When using the double-barrelled rifles against big and dangerous game . . . I find that a single trigger is a vast improvement on the old double trigger, for, apart from eliminating the risk of a bruised finger, the single trigger is indefinitely quicker, enabling a double shot to be placed almost simultaneously, if necessary. I have used the single trigger for some years and would on no account go back to the double."

Not all Westley Richards double guns are droplocks and fewer than a hundred have yet been chambered in .577 Nitro Express, but

Hemingway's was both. He could have found no better example of a top-quality, heavy-duty "stopping" rifle than this. Such guns never become obsolete and, with care, will last indefinitely.

With one exception, the "big guns" that Hemingway refers to in his safari writing are big-bore doubles—that is, rifles with two single-shot barrels, side by side, that fire fingertip-size bullets and deliver energy measured in tons. They are designed specifically for dangerous game and there is no faster way to fire two aimed shots:

*G.C. had taken her up closer than anyone but a great shot had a right to take her. If the lion had charged when she hit him G.C. would have had time for only one shot before the lion would have been on them. His big gun was as deadly and efficient if the lion came as it was a handicap if he had to shoot it at two and three hundred yards.*[1]

For G.C. and Mary Hemingway to be so close to a lion that Zaphiro "would have had time for only one shot" meant that they were at a distance the cat could have covered in two or three seconds in a charge—no more than 60 yards. At such close quarters Mary, an erratic shot, should have been able to hit this trophy she had been after for months. Even with Hemingway as backup on one side, G.C. was trading on his own skill and experience to give Mary the best possible opportunity. His "big gun" was a .470 Nitro Express. No matter how good he was with it—as a game pro-

*Hemingway holds the Rothschild/Percival takedown 6.5mm Mannlicher-Schoenauer that Mary used in East Africa while one of gunbearers poses the big single-trigger Westley Richards, which may have been a backup gun on this lion kill. The cartridges in Papa's vest appear to be for the .577.*

Earl Theisen/John F. Kennedy Library

fessional who did control work on marauding animals, he surely was expert—the stout recoil from the first shot would have kicked the muzzles upward nearly a foot and shoved him backward slightly. Still, he should have been able to fire the second barrel accurately inside of three seconds.

A double rifle differs greatly from a single-barrel repeater such as a bolt-action. Think of it as two guns on one stock; if one fails, there's still the other. It is also more akin to a fine shotgun, a balanced and often custom-fitted weapon that can perform brilliantly in certain situations and in certain hands. Depending on caliber, it weighs typically 10 to 16 pounds, almost twice as much as a conventional rifle, but it should come to the shoulder and swing effortlessly and shoot where it's pointed—i.e., where the shooter is looking. (Aiming is deliberate; pointing is instinctive.) Proper stock fit and balance not only improve shooting; along with sheer mass, they also reduce felt recoil and muzzle jump, which can be severe with big calibers. Big-bore double rifles usually have rudimentary open sights and rarely are fitted with scopes or carrying slings. A bolt-action rifle generally is better suited to deliberate shooting against a distant, barely moving target; a double shines when the target is close and moving fast.

Some professional hunters' skills with their double rifles became legendary, but the most extraordinary bag ever made with one occurred not in Africa but in Europe, during the First World War. In 1929 Dick Cooper (who would become a friend of Hemingway's) was dining one evening at the home of his hunting partner Bror Blixen at Babati, in Tanganyika. The guest of honor was Ernst Udet, the famous German fighter pilot, who was hunting with Blixen. The conversation came around to the merits of different guns and calibers. Cooper told this story:

"Talking of guns, when I was fighting in France in '17, our trenches were repeatedly attacked by German aircraft swooping in low over the defences. Their machine gun fire was devastating—of course we were sitting ducks.

For some reason I had my .450 Holland & Holland with me and thought I'd try it out on those buggers!

"Nothing to lose. The first one came straight for us, the pilot clearly visible hunched behind his machine gun. I fired some way in front and to my surprise he plummetted down like a pheasant behind me. The second the same. Hardly believing my luck and cheered on by the men, I quickly reloaded and got a shot off at the third just as he passed over. He also went down."

The dinner-table conviviality cooled somewhat, for it turned out that the three had been members of Udet's unit; until then, he had not known what became of them.[2]

Like double-barreled shotguns, double rifles break open in the middle. Pushing a thumb lever on top unlocks a hinge and lets the barrels pivot downward, which exposes the breeches. The empty shells pop out mechanically; the shooter drops a cartridge into each barrel and closes the gun again. This recocks the hammers, so now the gun is good to go. An experienced shooter can do this without conscious thought and without looking, in the dark or even at a trot. Often he will have the two fresh rounds ready between the fingers of his off hand.

An expert needs six-plus seconds to cycle the action and fire a second well-placed shot from a heavy-recoiling bolt-action rifle. If more than two shots are needed, the big-bore bolt rifle, with its typical four-round capacity (one in the chamber and three in the

*A photo that never made it into* Look. *Evidently the point was to impress the viewer with the cigar-size cartridges of the 13-pound .577 NE. Staring down the bores was like looking through the barrels of a 28-gauge shotgun.*

Earl Theisen/John F. Kennedy Library

magazine), would seem to have the edge over a double. However, someone like G.C. can reload a double, using the two spare rounds in his fingers, in less than five seconds and then fire those shots in three more seconds, for a total of less than 12 seconds—while the bolt-action man needs 20 seconds for his four rounds. (And forget about reloading a bolt rifle quickly under pressure.) The difference can seem like eternity when a Cape buffalo or elephant is in one's shorts.

The capacity to put big bullets rapidly and

accurately onto a fast-approaching target has to be backed up by fail-safe mechanical reliability; every possibility for malfunction must be removed. As Jim Sutherland pointed out, on safari the nearest gunsmith is more than a taxi-ride distant and breakdowns are at best highly inconvenient and at worst life-threatening.

Double rifles have always been astonishingly expensive because they require a great deal of handcraftsmanship to make. Bolt-action rifles can be mass-produced and so are an order of magnitude less costly. In the mid-1930s a largely handmade, "best"-grade heavy English double rifle cost about £170, equivalent to $850 or about 15 times as much as an American factory-made bolt-action sporting rifle. (Never mind that before 1956 no American gunmakers offered rifles of similar power.) Twenty years later, at the time of Hemingway's second safari, the same rifle cost £325 but, thanks to a much stronger post-war American economy, this was worth only about $910. Still, the importer's markup roughly doubled this, and in 1955 America $1,800 would buy a new Ford or Chevrolet. (Today, the price of a new London double rifle will buy a top-of-the-range Mercedes-Benz.)

Many African professional hunters who take clients after the Big Five—leopard, lion, Cape buffalo, rhino, elephant; game animals that "run both ways"—scrape together the cash for a heavy double, even if second-hand. It's insurance. Whatever the client is armed with, the PH, who as backup should shoot only when things go wrong, needs a big stopper that is ultra-reliable and fast-shooting: *If you make a fool of yourself all that you get is mauled but the white hunter who has a client wounded or killed loses, or seriously impairs, his livelihood.*[3]

As Hemingway also understood, a double rifle is a relatively short-range weapon. This is due to inherent limitations in accuracy, not because of its caliber or cartridge. Persuading one rifle barrel to shoot consistently to the very same place is difficult enough; regulating two barrels to do it together is not possible. (There are complex issues involving barrel "flip," bullet speed and even rifling twist, plus the fact that the barrel tubes converge somewhere downrange.) Instead, a heavy double should put its two bullets well within a hand-span at 50 yards. Since an inch one way or the other is almost irrelevant in the matter of killing anything larger than a prairie dog, for a hunter shooting offhand at close range this is more than adequate. Long-range accuracy is moot anyway, because dangerous game should be attacked inside 100 yards, to make it easier to place the bullet and then keep tabs on the beast after it's been hit.

Mechanically, the double gun has changed little since about 1875—not coincidentally, the date of Anson & Deeley's seminal action patent; it is a design that has proven itself. If the bolt-action .30-06 is the most popular hunting rifle, with the widest variety of uses, the heavy double is the rarest of all, produced in very small numbers for a narrow set of circumstances that only a handful of hunters ever encounter. In Hemingway's day few

*Cuba, 1942. Winston Guest, second (?) owner of the .577 Westley Richards but here cradling what looks like a pigeon gun, accepting a trophy at the Club des Cazadores from Martha Gellhorn Hemingway. Both charming and charmed, Winston Frederick Churchill Guest was a career playboy, although with a law degree from Columbia. His father Freddie was a prominent English peer, military officer and politician, as well as a racing driver, pilot, big-game hunter and first cousin of Winston Churchill; his mother was a Phipps, of America's industrial and philanthropic aristocracy. Guest became a top-ranked polo player and a well-traveled sportsman. He and Hemingway met in Kenya in 1933, where Guest was hunting with Bror Blixen, ex-husband of "Isak Dinesen," who had hired Beryl Markham to spot elephant for them from her airplane. (Read "I May Have to Shoot Him" in Markham's* West with the Night.*) After World War II, "Wolfie"—Ernest's nickname for Guest—got Hemingway onto Gardiners Island, the fabulous private shooting preserve his family had leased at the eastern end of Long Island. (Blixen appeared there as well; in 1938 the Guest family hired him to restore the island's bird population.) In 1947, in the Finca Vigía and with Hemingway as his best man, Winston married Boston beauty Lucille Douglas Cochrane, who became the fashion icon and socialite Ceezee Guest.*

John F. Kennedy Library

Americans had ever seen such a rifle—a product of British and European makers whose clients visited colonies in Asia and Africa—much less owned one. American big game was deer in the East, elk in the Rocky Mountains, and bear and moose up north, and none of these requires such formidable weaponry.

On his first safari, in 1933-'34, before he came by the .577 Westley Richards, Hemingway had with him a .470 Nitro Express double rifle (the same caliber that Zaphiro carried 20 years later). In letters to both Milford Baker and Mike Strater, Hemingway had mentioned the possibility of acquiring double rifles secondhand in Nairobi or Mombasa. Leicester Hemingway wrote: "Through Mr. Percival came the information that the guns, especially big-game rifles, were to be rented at a moderate rate" . . . Ernest's terse reply: 'I'll own my own guns. I don't want to rent them.' Ernest decided to put off all gun selection until he had reached Paris. He could go to the good armorers there and be outfitted for the expedition that was ahead of him and Pauline!" [4]

But, Leicester added, "Paris had been disappointing as a city in which to buy ideal weapons for African game. They had stuck with their lighter-weight American equipment, adding a .256 Mannlicher rifle with very little recoil as a fine gun for Pauline to shoot." [4]

Whether Ernest bought secondhand (and then returned at the end of the safari) or rented his .470, it likely came from Shaw & Hunter, Nairobi's famous gunshop—the very

store, now known as Kenya Bunduki, that unknowingly sold his Colt Woodsman pistol 65 years later.

Hemingway much preferred his .30-06 Springfield, which he said he liked to use "as a surgeon uses his scalpel" [5] but he recognized the .470's greater shocking power. The ideal calibers for big double rifles are the unique Nitro Express cartridges developed in Britain around 1900 that generate massive shock and—with the right bullets—can penetrate the thickest skin, muscle and bone. By the 1930s, when Hemingway was introduced to them in East Africa, they were already time-tested killers whose every detail (there are many, including the volume, length and shape of the case as well as the thickness of its wall and rim; the type of gunpowder and the resultant chamber pressure; and the weight, shape and composition of the bullet) had been refined for performance and dependability in double rifles.

By 1850 a London gunmaker named James (the Younger) Purdey had applied the term "Express Train" to his muzzleloading sporting rifles to equate them to the powerful, high-speed trains that were then beginning to crisscross Great Britain. The label caught on, was shortened to "Express" and, in the 1870s and '80s, was applied to self-contained cartridges such as the .450 BPE (Black Powder Express) developed for the new breechloading guns. Blackpowder ammunition throws out a cloud of smoke that usually obscures the target for a few critical seconds. In 1884 came nitrocellulose gunpowder, which was not only smokeless, but it also made much more energy and thereby drove a bullet faster and harder. This led to an entirely new series of cartridges dubbed Nitro Express, which revolutionized big-game hunting. To get power adequate to stop elephant and such, blackpowder rifles had to be of enormous calibers, or bore diameters, which made them extremely heavy and cumbersome, and along with the thick smoke came fearsome recoil that sometimes broke collarbones and gunstocks. Nitro Express rifles, even double-barreled ones, weighed half as much as the blackpowder monsters, made no smoke, were far easier to shoot and yet were more powerful.

The first of the Nitro Express cartridges was the .450, introduced by the London firm of J. Rigby & Co. in 1898. It became an immediate success with sportsmen traveling to Africa and Asia. Unfortunately for Rigby, however, and others who adopted that cartridge, in 1899 the British government of India began to regulate .450-caliber ammunition, with significant consequences for hunters.

This was the height of the Victorian Era, when British troops in colonies and protectorates around the globe were perennially on guard against revolt by indigenous people who somehow failed to appreciate the benevolent hand of the Monarch. Nowhere was this more so than in India, the crown jewel of Britain's holdings, and especially on "the Frontier," where northwestern India—now Pakistan—and Afghanistan came together. This was England's Wild West, where the "wily Pathan" was engaged in the national pastime

of making life tough for the infidel. Turning the invader's own weapons, stolen or copied, against him was a favored modus operandi. (Little has changed in that part of the world.)

Bombay Castle's main concern was a .450-caliber cartridge used in the single-shot Martini-Henry service rifle. Millions of rounds and thousands of these rifles were already in India. The army was ordered to physically account for every single cartridge and empty case, whether expended in the field or at target practice, to try to prevent them falling into the hands of hostiles. By 1902 the legislation had been expanded to prohibit anyone visiting India from bringing .450 rifles or ammunition, sporting or military, with them. Since virtually every British gunmaker was building rifles for the many .450 cartridges then available and since India was still the British sportsman's Mecca (East Africa's glory days came after WWI), this caused considerable fuss back home.

With the favored .450 now illegal in its best market, British firms rushed to make cartridges of different calibers. The first decade of the 20th Century saw a burst of ballistic inventiveness in the UK that rivaled what happened in the US when the .30-06 hit the civilian market: Gunmakers trotted out new Nitro Express cartridges right and left. All but one—among them the .450, .465, .470, .475, .500, .577 and .600—were developed between 1898 and about 1905 for double or single-shot rifles. (The exception, the .700 NE, an exercise in one-upmanship, appeared in 1988.) The most popular proved to be the

.470 Nitro Express. Its diameter made it a rule-beater; it used smokeless Cordite (a form of nitroglycerine) propellant; and, generating more than 5,000 foot-pounds of energy at the muzzle, it was an "express train" by any standard. Despite the larger caliber, however, its performance did not exceed that of the .450 NE, which did not completely disappear. It was never illegal in Africa and many .450s wound up there when that continent became a popular hunting ground for Europeans.

*I was so surprised by the way he had rolled over dead from the shot after we had been prepared for a charge, for heroics, and for drama, that I felt more let down than pleased. It was our first lion and we were very ignorant and this was not what we had paid to see. Charo and M'Cola both shook P.O.M.'s hand and then Charo came over and shook hands with me.*

*"Good shot, B'wana," he said in Swahili. "Piga m'uzuri."*

*"Did you shoot, Karl?" I asked.*

*"No. I was just going to when you shot."*

*"You didn't shoot him, Pop?"*

*"No. You'd have heard it." He opened the breech and took out the two big .450 No.2's.* [6]

The .450 No. 2, Pop's stopping-rifle caliber, was a variant invented by W.J. Jeffery & Company, of London, to overcome some early pressure and extraction problems in the .450 Nitro Express (which were quickly solved anyway). Although its performance is identical, the cartridge itself is significantly larger than the .450 NE's and that may account for its popularity with some professional hunters of that era: Bigger must be better!

On the other hand, they may simply have found older secondhand rifles at affordable prices, beggars not being choosers. Or as working professionals they may have opted for the No. 2 early on, to avoid the initial problems of the Rigby original. Or sometimes a grateful (and wealthy) client presents his professional hunter with a rifle as a gift—and this is likely to be an older gun or a spare. However, it seems none of these reasons applied to Percival, who owned a matched pair of .450 No. 2 rifles made by Jos. Lang & Son, London, which (company records indicate) he bought new on 9 December 1927. In any event, the .450 No. 2 was and remains every bit as effective as the Nitro Express version, only a bit bigger and bulkier.

*I sat down, the big gun feeling heavy and unfamiliar, held on the buff's shoulder, squeezed off and flinched without firing. Instead of the sweet clean pull of the Springfield with the smooth, unhesitant release at the end, this trigger came to what, in a squeeze, seemed metal stuck against metal. It was like when you shoot in a nightmare. I couldn't squeeze it and I corrected from my flinch, held my breath, and pulled the trigger. It pulled off with a jerk and the big gun made a rocking explosion out of which I came, seeing the buffalo still on his feet, and going out of sight to the left in a climbing run, to let off the second barrel and throw a burst of rock dust and dirt over his hind quarters. He was out of shot before I could reload the double-barreled .470 and we had all heard the snorting and crashing of another rhino that had gone out of the lower end of the reeds and on un-*

*der the heavy trees on our side without showing more than a glimpse of his bulk in the reeds.* [6]

The trigger is a critical element of a rifle. If it can't be relied upon for a precise, predictable let-off, accuracy suffers greatly—as Hemingway demonstrates. He doesn't identify the maker, but on an East African safari of the 1930s any .470 was surely a British-made double rifle. The problem Hemingway describes—"metal stuck against metal"—could stem from faulty manufacture. Unlikely, in a costly, handcrafted rifle. Alternatively, a tiny steel burr or even a sliver of stock wood could have drifted into the lockwork and bound it up. Or the action screws might have been over-tightened—perhaps by a provincial gunsmith doing routine maintenance—which also can cause the lockwork to bind. With poor care and only occasional use, a backup gun might even become rusty inside. And this was, as noted, apparently a rented gun. But the most likely cause, and the one that professional hunters immediately think of when they read this passage, was that in the heat of the moment Hemingway simply forgot to slip off the safety; the triggers were blocked.

Most doubles—rifles and shotguns—have the safety catch on the top of the stock wrist, right at the shooter's hand, and most of these engage automatically when the gun is opened for loading. An experienced double-gunner instinctively slides the button forward, off, with his thumb as he raises the gun to his shoulder. (The safety catches of Hemingway's most familiar guns—his bolt-action Springfield rifle and pump-action Winchester shotgun—lie in

very different places, and they do not engage automatically.) This was a classic blunder that can be embarrassing or, in a charge, fatal to the shooter. Hemingway chose not to explain it—or he may not even have been aware of what he'd done. Eventually he got off a shot and then had no difficulty firing the second barrel; he'd figured out the problem and deactivated the safety.

A safety catch may seem to be a minor feature, but clearly its function is critical, especially with dangerous game; even any noise it might make can be important. In *Under Kilimanjaro* (48) the author and Pop have a surprise encounter with a lion at close range. Hemingway wrote:

*"And I heard your safety click and I was surprised that you would have a safety that clicked."*

*"What an observant type," Pop said. "I don't think it did click, actually, I think you made that up."*

*"It clicked."*

The point is that a mechanical sound, however faint, is so alien in a natural environment that it not only alerts the game, but it may also—in a staring contest with a lion, for instance—provoke a nasty reaction. A safety catch on any hunting rifle should slide on or off positively but silently.

Between his two safaris, Ernest had at least one more memorable encounter with a double rifle. In January of 1950, he and Mary were visiting friends near Treviso, in northern Italy. Mary reported that she had stepped outside after lunch and found the family's sons trying to ring the bell in the tower of the estate's chapel by hitting the clapper with a .22 rifle. One thing led to another and soon out came more guns, including a "heavy .477 with its twenty-five-year-old ammunition."[7] Whether this was a typo for a .577 or a .470 hardly matters; Bianca Franchetti, the matron of the family, instructed Ernest to shoot the statues atop the back wing of the carriage house with it. "We're replacing them with better ones of marble," she said. "Do shoot them. Bring them down." Mary wrote that Ernest shot at one and missed, intentionally, she thought.

According to Westley Richards' records, No. 17425 was built for one S.H. Christy, of Plaish Hall, Church Stretton, Salop, as "a double hammerless detachable-lock, single-trigger full-load .577 rifle." It was completed in October 1913, but Stephen Henry Christy may never have used it.

At the age of 23, in 1902, Christy had gotten a taste of southern Africa as a staff officer of the 20th Hussars, a cavalry regiment, in the Boer War. He was wounded, won the Distinguished Service Order and was mentioned in dispatches. After a posting to Nigeria, he returned home, resigned the army, married and lived a well-to-do country squire's life in peaceful Shropshire. Church Stretton is barely 30 miles west of Birmingham, the home of Westley Richards. He likely ordered the big rifle as part of a plan to return to Africa for safari. It is not something he would have hunted with at home, or even in India, as it is too powerful for all but the largest African game.

However, his beloved wife died in November 1913, a month after the rifle was finished; and the following summer began the Great War. Christy rejoined his regiment, which went straightaway into combat in France. On 3 September 1914, Captain Stephen Christy was killed in the run-up to the first Battle of the Marne. French villagers with whom he had struck up a friendship buried him and his mare, Kitty, in a field some 30 miles from Paris. He was 35 years old.

The Christys had no children. How the valuable .577 came to Winston Guest is not yet known, but Guest apparently had it in East Africa in 1933, when he and Ernest Hemingway met. Guest still had it when he traveled to Cuba in September 1942, ostensibly to check on his family's mining interests there. He stayed on the island and wound up second-in-command of the Crook Factory, Hemingway's makeshift counterintelligence ring charged with keeping an eye out for Axis agents. Cuba, barely 90 miles from the American mainland, had a huge population of expatriate Spaniards, many of whom had been Falangists in their recent Civil War and thus were suspected of Nazi sympathies. This was of grave concern to the Federal Bureau of Investigation, which in 1942 was—like much of the American government—still on its back foot when it came to fighting the world war. Spruille Braden, the new American ambassador in Havana, recruited Hemingway—affluent, active and connected at all levels of island society—to help in the interim. Papa accepted with enthusiasm. Never one to think small, Hemingway soon conceived of a new and

*The Christy/Guest/Hemingway .577 today is displayed (along with Hemingway photos and as-sorted memorabilia) behind glass at the Curry Mansion Inn, a bed & breakfast on Caroline Street in Key West, midway between Sloppy Joe's Bar and the Hemingway house.*    Steve Helsley

more aggressive sort of clandestine warfare.

The Caribbean, the Gulf of Mexico and the southeast coast of the US were then infested with German U-boats that were picking off tankers delivering fuel from refineries in New Orleans and Aruba to Britain, fighting for its life against the Nazi onslaught. Up and down the Atlantic seaboard, American yachtsmen were answering the call to assist the US Navy in patrolling for German raiders and infiltrators. Hemingway would go them one better:

With official connivance, he was able to arm *Pilar*, his sportfisherman, with light machine guns, a bazooka, explosives and military-spec radio gear, and obtain precious gasoline. Then he shifted some of his anti-spy-squad irregulars to the boat as crew.

Enemy submarines sometimes bought or seized fresh food from small boats. Hemingway's plan was to pose as fishermen and to lure a U-boat to *Pilar*'s side, then sweep its deck with gunfire while two of his Basque jai-alai-player pals lofted a satchel charge into its conning tower. Winston Guest contributed his participation and, Patrick Hemingway recalled, his elephant rifle. Hemingway had been disappointed to find that his boat couldn't take the pounding recoil of the .50-caliber machine guns he'd hoped to mount; maybe, he and Wolfie speculated, the Westley's 750-grain solid-nose bullets might punch through the skin of a U-boat! [8]

Fortunately for all concerned, and for American literature, in months of cruising as a Q-ship, *Pilar* never encountered a submarine, at least at close range. The Navy eventually took its radios back, but some of the weaponry stayed on board for years. Finally, in the spring of 1958, with armed revolution looming in Cuba, Ernest and Gregorio Fuentes, his captain, took the boat far offshore and dumped over the side "heavy rifles, sawed-off shotguns, hand grenades and canisters and belts of ammunition for automatic rifles I had never known existed aboard *Pilar*," Mary Hemingway wrote. The Westley Richards, of course, was not one of these; by then, it had gone on safari for at least the second time in its history, with Ernest and Mary from September 1953 into January 1954.

Hemingway preferred bolt-action rifles, specifically his Griffin & Howe Springfield and the Mannlicher-Schoenauers, and his experience with the .470's balky triggers 20 years earlier may have soured him on doubles, but no hunter is immune to the romance of these super-specialized, costly and deadly works of art. By their very nature, they proclaim "Africa!" as nothing else can. Papa owned the Westley Richards rifle anyway; he would not have left it behind when he returned to Kenya. Its later history is still somewhat patchy, but it seems to have remained temporarily in Nairobi when the Hemingways departed. ("The Beretta S3 Over/Under.") Eventually, it was returned to Hemingway.

The Westley Richards surfaced next in Key West when, reportedly, a member of the Thompson family, fallen upon hard times, sold it. Charles Thompson and Ernest had been close friends, and Charles, an enthusiastic hunter and fisherman, accompanied Ernest and Pauline on the first safari. (He appears in *Green Hills of Africa* as "Karl.") Ernest apparently gave or sold him the rifle. Charles Thompson returned to Africa with his wife Lorine and shot at least one elephant; and his home in Key West was known for its large gun cabinet and hunting trophies. The rifle was next sold, in the early 1970s, to the son of the present owner for $2,800.

Today, somewhat battered and with its leather case and cleaning equipment, the big Westley is on display at the Curry Mansion Inn in Key West. The faded cardboard tag attached to the handle of the case bears Ernest Hemingway's name and "S.S. *Flandre*"—the ship on which the Hemingways sailed from New York to Le Havre en route to Africa in June of 1953.

# THREE (FOUR?)
# COLT WOODSMAN PISTOLS

*I always shot scorpions with the .22 pistol.*     —*Under Kilimanjaro, page 272*

In July of 1919, six months after returning from the ambulance corps in northern Italy, Ernest Hemingway invited two friends he'd made there to Michigan for a camping trip. In a letter, he was specific in his instructions about the fishing gear and ammunition they should have, and he added that he would bring along a 20-gauge shotgun and a .32-caliber pistol as well as a .22 rifle and pistol. He promised plenty of shooting.

The shotgun may have been the one he received from his grandfather for his 10th birthday, 10 years earlier. The .32 was never mentioned again. Of .22 rifles, he owned several in his lifetime. And this is the first mention of the .22 handgun: a Colt Automatic Pistol, Target model—later dubbed the Woodsman. It appears in the photograph on page 110, which may have been taken on this very camping trip. Although we have not found its serial number in the Hemingway archives, we believe it was 12072, thus made (according to Colt records) circa 1919. It was the first of a number of Woodsmans that Hemingway

would eventually own.

During a long and fruitful correspondence with Ian Parker, who had been a game warden in Kenya in the 1950s and '60s and had known both Philip Percival and Denis Zaphiro, who figured so prominently in Hemingway's African writing, it came out that Parker had once found a certain .22 pistol for sale in Nairobi. In an e-mail to author Calabi, he wrote:

"I was with a fellow Game Warden—Rodney Elliott (deceased). We happened to be going through the gun store (once called Shaw & Hunter, subsequently Kenya Bunduki) in or around 1997/8 when we came across the pistol. Rodney was something of a gun buff, saw it and without hesitation said 'That is the .22 that Hemingway gave to Denis Zaphiro.' It merely had a tag with a ledger number on it. I was sufficiently impressed to go back to the desk and ask to look at the ledger: it had been deposited in 1996 by Pat Smith (DZ's minder) in the name of Zaphiro. Well, that didn't prove that EH gave the weapon to DZ, but it certainly proved that Elliott had recognised the

*With fly rod, knife and handgun. Ernest Hemingway in Michigan around 1920, perhaps on the camping trip with his fellow WWI veterans. The shoulder rig holds what is likely his first .22-caliber Colt Automatic Pistol, Serial No. 12072—made in 1919 and then found and lost again in Kenya 80 years later.*

John F. Kennedy Library

weapon. How did he know that it had come from EH? He must have been told by DZ. They knew one another well and had joined the Game Department at around the same time. As I recall, Rodney's further comment was to the effect that 'If anyone knew that had been a Hemingway gun, it wouldn't be lying there. It must be worth a lot of money!' I had no ground for challenging Rodney's certainty, but then there is the Firearms Certificate!

"[A]s supporting evidence . . . it was a very strange weapon for a Game Warden to want or have. All the handguns which I knew [to be] owned by Wardens were in the law-enforcer's calibres: .32 (only 1) upwards. Most [of us] thought .38s were on the light side and several had .45s. In my mind, Sufuria [*Zaphiro's nickname*] owning what at very best was a 'plinker' would have been far more for the sentimental reason of having been given it by a special friend, than as a working tool—which is why he had firearms. He was never a target shooter and even less was he a pistol shot."

In August 2009 Parker followed up with a visit to the Police Firearms Bureau in Nairobi, where the director found Denis Zaphiro's files, and in them papers for a Colt Woodsman, Serial No. 12072. The pistol had been registered to Zaphiro on 12 July 1954; in 1996 it was turned over to the police for safekeeping by Pat Smith, the neighbor of Zaphiro's who had been taking care of him as he descended into Alzheimer's; and then the pistol was consigned to Kenya Bunduki for sale to

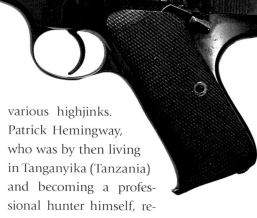

*The young Hemingway's first Colt .22 pistol, thought to bear Serial No. 12072 and thus made in 1919, would have resembled this one—a First Series Target model with a slanted grip and a six- or 6⅝-inch round "pencil" barrel.* Larry Carter

recover storage costs. And there Parker and Elliott spotted it.

Ernest and Mary Hemingway departed Kenya on 11 March 1954 after more than six months in East Africa. They had become notably fond of Denis Zaphiro, and he of them. (In 1957, Zaphiro would spend almost four months as a guest of the Hemingways in Cuba and the US.) The circumstances were unusual: When Philip Percival, who had come out of retirement for the Hemingways' safari, returned home, the Game Department either

assigned Zaphiro to look after them or closed an eye to his attaching himself to their safari. (A professional hunter named Roy Home had been seconded to Percival for this important client, but Hemingway reportedly disliked him and ran him off.) Hemingway, now middle-aged, could truly take the "Papa" role with Zaphiro, who was young enough to be one of his sons, while admiring his professional skill with guns and game. In addition to serving as their safari minder, de facto or official, Zaphiro supported Mary in her attempts to become a hunter and joined her husband in various highjinks.

Patrick Hemingway, who was by then living in Tanganyika (Tanzania) and becoming a professional hunter himself, recalled that he and his father would go out at night in the hunting car, with Zaphiro—nicknamed the "Stirling Moss of the Land Rover" as well as "G.C."—at the wheel, to chase nocturnal spring hares and shoot at them with the Woodsman. On one occasion, Papa was bounced right out of the open car. Hemingway also used the pistol on camp pests such as jackals and even scorpions crawling out of the firewood. Evidently, at the end of the safari, Hemingway presented it to Zaphiro. Papa was a notably generous man who formed strong bonds with many "ordinary" people, particularly hunters. Considering how often the Colt had appeared in his life, and then later in *Under Kilimanjaro*, this was a meaningful gift.

It's interesting to connect the dots between the first mention of the Woodsman, in 1919, and its brief, serendipitous reappearance in Nairobi almost 80 years later. Leicester Hemingway wrote that his older brother had shot pike with it in the River Marne, in France in 1922. In May 1930 Ernest mentioned it in a letter to Milford Baker, who was advising him on the details of his .30-06 rifle from Griffin & Howe. Along with the Model 12 Winchester, it survived the fire in the Pfeiffers' barn in 1931. On 9 February 1932 Hemingway wrote to Mike Strater that he intended to bring the Colt .22 to Africa on his first safari. (But there is no mention of it in *Green Hills of Africa*, the book that came out of that trip.) On 7 April 1935 Hemingway accidentally shot himself with it aboard *Pilar*. He was trying to kill a shark that had been dragged into the cockpit. The fish thrashed, the gaff broke and Hemingway's shot went wide. The little bullet struck a metal rail and came apart, and the fragments ricocheted into his left leg.

*I*n *the old days we never carried pistols and it would have been very bad form in the days when we were pukka sahibs. But now you put the pistol on as naturally as you buttoned the flap of your trousers. . . . It was a Colt Match Woodsman .22 caliber shooting high-speed hollow-point ammunition. It was very deadly and you could hit what you shot at and there were ten rounds in each clip. I carried two extra clips in a small plastic bag in the right-hand pocket of my bush jacket and carried the extra ammunition in a screw top, wide-mouth medicine bottle which had held liver capsules. This bottle had held fifty red-and-white capsules and now held sixty-five rounds of hollow points.* [1]

The second of Hemingway's safaris took place when Kenya was in the midst of the Mau Mau Uprising. This was an anti-European rebellion by a secret society of the Kikuyu, a people who had during 60 years of British rule been increasingly destabilized and driven off their tribal lands onto white-owned farms or into the slums of Nairobi. The terrorism began in 1952 and grew into a colonial nightmare, spawning fears of the sort of revolt Britain had encountered in 1857 in India. The Mau Mau leadership devised elaborate "oathing" ceremonies to bind people to its cause. These evolved into gruesome rituals of blood, religion and sex that strongly affected the tribal people and fed whites' most lurid anxieties. In reality, only some 32 white civilians died at the hands of Mau Mau, but the notion that trusted family servants and farmhands could rise up in slaughter at any moment turned Kenya inside out. Units of the KAR (the King's African Rifles) and the Kenya Regiment were mobilized; a militia was raised; settlers organized freelance commando raids; and thousands of regular troops were sent from Britain, along with a detachment of Royal Marines and the cruiser

HMS *Kenya*. In attempts to root out insurgent camps in the Aberdare Mountains, the Royal Air Force even carried out WWII-style carpet-bombing attacks. Officially, 10,527 Mau Mau were reported killed in action—largely by bush-savvy Kenya and Tribal Police and the loyalist Kikuyu Home Guard, both black and white. Naturally, among the most valuable of these fighters were professional hunters and game wardens, who swapped their sporting rifles for Stens and Webleys and went out,

self-defense against Mau Mau was absolutely miniscule. There was a huge element of machismo involved and, to a degree, it was the last flaring of Hollywood's wild west image. They say that there were more killed in handgun accidents in bars during those years than the Mau Mau ever took out. While apocryphal, for I have never seen any statistics, it encapsulates an element of truth, certainly in the bar-room revelry that characterized those years. I was present at incidents that were hi-

Colt No. 128866-S, one of the two Second Series (1947-'55) Woodsman models bought by Hemingway at Abercrombie & Fitch en route to Europe and then East Africa in June 1953. The other one, No. 118929-S, would have been identical.

Brad Stanley/John Cymbal: Driven

often with their native trackers, to hunt men instead of the Big Five.

Kenyan whites took to carrying guns everywhere—"now you put the pistol on as naturally as you buttoned the flap of your trousers"—including into Nairobi on social occasions or shopping trips. Ian Parker recalled:

"Of the thousands [of handguns] carried, I imagine that the number actually used in

lariously funny (at least to those taking part), when guns instead of darts were fired at dartboards and a bottle or two was blown off the shelves behind the bar."

The Mau Mau Emergency peaked in 1954, while the Hemingways were in-country, and then sputtered on into 1959. If Hemingway truly brought his little pistol to Kenya for protection, he didn't take the terrorist threat seriously. His Model 12 shotgun would have

*The right-hand ledger page recording Abercrombie & Fitch Colt Woodsman sales for 1953. Hemingway's name appears three times in the "Buyer" column, for pistols No. 128866 and 118929, bought under his own name, and then just above Wm. Lowe. (Serial numbers are on the preceding left-hand page, not shown; the sales clerk left off the "-S" suffix, which appeared on all post-WWII Woodsman serial numbers.) Evidently all three Colts—Lowe's and Hemingway's—were to be shipped to Hemingway's post-office box in Nairobi.* Griffin & Howe

been far better than any handgun as a close-quarters defense weapon (and he mentions tucking it under his cot at night, although this is standard procedure in any safari camp against troublesome lion, leopard or hyena). More likely Hemingway brought his pistol just for fun and took the rebellion as an excuse to wear it as part of his Bwana persona.

The uprising seriously dented East African tourism. To try to undo some of the bad publicity with upbeat stories in American magazines (which Hemingway provided), the Kenyan government assisted the Hemingways by opening, for their safari alone, a game reserve in the Kajiado District. They also hunted in the adjacent district, called Machakos. These were Masai and Wakamba tribal lands

south and east of Nairobi. Mau Mau activity was mostly in the central highlands, north of the city, and was nearly all Kikuyu. There is a Mau Mau "scare" in *Under Kilimanjaro* and *True at First Light* when escaped insurgents are thought to be heading toward the safari camp, but Hemingway makes light of it by poking fun at the earnest young British policeman who brings the news in a cloud of Land Rover dust. In reality, according to Ian Parker, "Southern Kajiado was hardly a Mau Mau area—so much so that, as at the coast, one left one's holstered weapon locked up in a safe."

In Africa Hemingway carried his pistol in a tooled-leather Abercrombie & Fitch holster with a leg tie-down—which Debba, his Kam-

*Hemingway, ever competitive, and* Look *editor Bill Lowe target-shooting in one of the safari camps with .22s—Papa with his Model 61 Winchester rifle, Lowe with a Woodsman pistol, presumably No. 128721, which he bought at A&F on 23 June '53 at 4:00 PM and had shipped to Nairobi.*

Earl Theisen/John F. Kennedy Library

ba "fiancée," caressed in *Under Kilimanjaro* and *True at First Light,* no doubt symbolically. (Note too Hemingway linking it to what's behind "the flap of your trousers." Another "friend and companion with secrets shared and triumphs and disasters not revealed as the other friend a man has all his life," like his Model 12?) Hemingway's comment that

*Hemingway wearing a holstered pistol in East Africa on his second safari—surely one of the two new Woodsmans he'd bought just before leaving New York. This photo closed "The Christmas Gift," the lengthy story that Hemingway wrote for* Look *Magazine (April 20 and May 4, 1954) about the two bush-plane crashes, on consecutive days, that he and Mary survived at the end of almost five months in the bush; thus, the editors chose this emotional image.* Earl Theisen/John F. Kennedy Library

"in the old days we never carried pistols" is a bit of a stretch for a man who, having been on safari only once before, 20 years earlier, could hardly claim to be an old Africa hand, but it is substantially correct. Normally handguns—pistols and revolvers—are not useful on safari. Some professionals carry them to finish off wounded game or for last-ditch protection against leopard or lion, but in general they're too inaccurate for meat hunting and not powerful enough for big game. In Kenya it was illegal to shoot game with a handgun.

Semi-automatic rifles and shotguns were illegal for civilians in mid-1950s Kenya, but semi-auto handguns were not. All semi-automatic pistols operate essentially the same way: Insert a loaded magazine into the grip; pull back the spring-loaded slide, which cocks the hammer; then release the slide, which, as it snaps forward, shoves the first cartridge into the chamber and locks everything up. Squeeze the trigger and the gun fires. The energy of the shot cycles the slide backward to eject the empty case and re-cock the hammer. The return spring then shoves the slide forward again, to scoop up a fresh round (rising from the magazine) and re-lock the action, ready for firing again. This happens in an eye-blink with each pull of the trigger until the magazine is empty—in the case of a Woodsman, 10 times.

There are three standard sizes of .22-caliber rimfire ammunition—Short, Long and Long Rifle—and any number of variants, many of which are now obsolete (BB, CB, Extra Long, WRF, WMR, Winchester Automatic and so on). The Woodsman was chambered only for the Long Rifle version, which despite its name is also used in pistols. That 65 of these cartridges fit into a bottle meant for 50 liver capsules indicates their size. The 40-grain bullet itself is smaller than an aspirin tablet. (The 750-grain slug in a .577 NE round is as large

77

+*● 77   ERNEST HEMINGWAY'S COLT MATCH TARGET WOODSMAN PISTOL, No.
128866S. Standard markings and finish. Checkered walnut grips. Excellent condition, retain-
ing 95% blue, 6 in. barrel, .22 (L.R) caliber. With its magazine. Now in a leather and velvet
display case by Arno Werner, master bookbinder, the lid inscribed in gold leaf 'Ernest
Hemingway's /Colt Woodsman Pistol/No. 128866S'. With its original A & F tooled leather
holster; and documents of authentication and interest (book illustrated above not included).

ILLUSTRATED
*Guns*, May 1981, cover and pp. 40-41 (color)
*Man at Arms*, Sept/Oct 1979, cover and p. 10 (color)

The accompanying documents trace the pistol's history from its shipment by Colt's to Abercrombie &
Fitch in March 1953; its sale by A & F to 'Mr. Ernest Hemingway... occupation: Author...' in June
1953 (the year in which Hemingway was awarded the Pulitzer Prize for *The Old Man and the Sea*); its
return from Hemingway's estate to A & F in 1964; thence to the present owner. Research on the subject
by Horace Greeley IV was published in *Guns* magazine, May 1981.

*DJ Bid $1850.⁰⁰          $3800.00
+10%  $4180.00*

After the death of its owner, No. 128866-S was consigned back to A&F, where in July 1963 it was
bought by an employee of the gun department. In the late 1970s Dr. Margaret Greeley bought it for
her husband, Horace Greeley IV. Horace researched the pistol and published his findings in both
Man at Arms *and* Guns. *In October 1981 it was sold again, at a landmark Christie's auction in
New York City. This page from the auction catalog records a wishful shopper's top bid and the final
gavel price plus buyer's premium. The pistol was auctioned again, by James D. Julia, in October
2007; with its holster and corroborating papers, it then made $10,925.*          David Trevallion

as the last joint of an adult finger.) The basic rimfire .22 has for more than a century been by far the best-selling of all cartridges and very widely used in both rifles and handguns. It costs just pennies per round, compared to as much as $25 each for the Nitro Express calibers, which makes it ideal for target practice. Just about every shooter who begins at an early age does so with a .22.

Thus Hemingway's Woodsman was a low-power weapon good only for "plinking"—informal target shooting—potting guinea fowl for the kitchen, or self-defense at arm's length. Self-defense against thin-skinned, thinking opponents, that is—humans who might be deterred by the threat of even a smallbore pistol:

*Now standing in one corner of a boxing ring with a .22 caliber Colt automatic pistol, shooting a bullet weighing only 40 grains and with a striking energy of only 51 foot pounds at 25 feet from the muzzle, I will guarantee to kill either Gene [Tunney] or Joe Louis before they can get to me from the opposite corner. This is the smallest caliber pistol cartridge made; but it is also one of the most accurate and easy to hit with, since the pistol has no recoil. I have killed many horses with it, cripples and for bear bait, with a single shot, and what will kill a horse will kill a man. . . . Yet this same pistol bullet fired at point-blank range will not even dent a grizzly's skull, and to shoot at a grizzly [bear] with a .22-caliber pistol would simply be one way of committing suicide.* [2]

As Hemingway points out, the near-total lack of recoil from a .22 pistol contributes to its accuracy, and it can be lethal on humans and even big animals. Anyone who expects to put down a horse or a man with a .22 would use a solid bullet, not a hollow-point, and shoot at very close range. Under these conditions a .22 can be destructive beyond expectation, because even the solid may break into fragments that go off in different directions through the tissue.

The firm that was founded in 1836 as The Patent Arms Manufacturing Company and reorganized as The Colt's Patent Firearms Manufacturing Company in 1854 first became famous for its Civil War revolvers, later known in the Old West as Peacemakers or Equalizers. (From the saying "God made men; Samuel Colt made men equal.") Then in 1911 came Colt's just-as-illustrious .45-caliber semi-auto pistol, which was carried by the American military through two world wars, Korea and Vietnam and is still in wide use today. As were Hemingway's Browning shotguns and this Colt Model 1911, the Woodsman was designed by the firearms genius John M. Browning, which virtually guaranteed high functioning.

On its debut, in 1915, it was simply called the Colt Automatic Pistol, Target Model, and it cost the substantial sum of $32, about $675 in 2010. The Woodsman name appeared in 1927 and stuck for the rest of the gun's production life, until 1977. A Woodsman is narrow and relatively lightweight and its grip is set at a rakish angle, like a Luger pistol's. The gun points naturally, which with its excellent trigger mechanism makes it unusually precise

*Idaho, November 1958. Papa wears a handgun on his hip while posing with A.E. Hotchner, who was visiting Ketchum to discuss the TV screenplay he was writing for* For Whom the Bell Tolls
. Lloyd Arnold/ John F. Kennedy Library

in offhand use. Many variations were made. Hemingway's "Match" version had a longer barrel for greater accuracy. Regardless of model or price, the mechanism was the same, while overall weight, barrel length and mass, grip styles, finishes and sights varied. The

Woodsman was a high-quality weapon and it is still popular today.

Hemingway liked the pistol enough to have owned at least three of them. The accompanying page from Abercrombie & Fitch's firearms ledgers records that Ernest Hemingway,

Author, bought two Woodsman pistols, Serial Nos. 128866-S and 118929-S, at 12:25 PM on 25 June 1953. His age is given incorrectly—he was then a month short of 54, not 55—and his address is listed as P.O. Box 557, Nairobi. Ernest and Mary sailed from New York aboard the SS *Flandre* for Le Havre later that same day, June 25th. In the middle of the page, Hemingway's name appears a third time, just above that of Wm. Lowe, age 32, who evidently had a charge account at A&F and who had himself bought a Woodsman two days earlier. Bill Lowe was the editor of *Look* Magazine. Not only had he outbid *Life* for the rights to a Hemingway story about the forthcoming safari, he had also arranged to hunt with the Hemingways in Africa. His pistol was to be sent to Hemingway's Kenya address as well. The second column from the right, headed "65C," probably indicates that all three Colts were to be shipped (by air, surely) to Kenya on July 29th, since Ernest and Mary would spend several weeks in France and Spain en route and wouldn't arrive at the port of Mombasa until 6 August. Ernest perhaps did not want to deal with three more guns while traveling; his original Colt .22, No. 12072, was no doubt securely packed away in one of the 46 pieces of luggage he and Mary brought aboard the ship.

Woodsman No. 12072 apparently stayed in Africa in the hands of Denis Zaphiro. The two newer pistols returned. After Hemingway's death, No. 128866-S was consigned back to A&F, where it was acquired by Joe Marchica, an employee of the gun department, in July 1963. In the late 1970s Dr. Margaret Greeley bought it for her husband, Horace Greeley IV, for his birthday. Greeley researched the pistol extensively and published his findings in both *Man at Arms* (September/October 1979) and *Guns* (May 1981) magazines. Thereafter it passed through at least two auction houses, its price as a Hemingway gun steadily increasing, and today it belongs to a Michigan sportsman and Hemingway aficionado.

For some years, it seems the third Woodsman, No. 118929-S, hung in a shadow box in the home of William W. Seward, a professor of English at Old Dominion University in Virginia. He, the bookish, retiring academic, and Hemingway, the gregarious outdoorsman who detested literary over-analysis, had an unlikely but mutually satisfying 20-year friendship. Seward wrote that the pistol had been given to him by Mary in 1963 as a memento of her husband's regard. [3] Professor Seward and his wife Florence had no children, and the whereabouts of the gun today are unknown.

Thus, three Hemingway Colt semi-auto .22 pistols. Or four? In a letter to his publisher, Charles Scribner, dated 22 July 1949 (the day after his 50th birthday) and sent from the Finca Vigía, his home outside Havana, Papa wrote:

*Had wonderful birthday presents: Juan Dunabeitia who served with me at sea in the war smuggled in a .22 Cal Colt Match Target pistol. Our priest gave me two bottles of Tequila.* [4]

The tequila might not have lasted the day. Who knows what happened to the pistol?

# THE MODEL 61 WINCHESTER & OTHER .22 RIFLES

*So out they all came: the lovely old Griffin & Howe Springfield of* Green Hills of Africa, *Pauline's little 6.5 Mannlicher, or that which literally done in poor Francis Macomber; a couple of .22 plinking rifles . . .*

—Lloyd Arnold, *High on the Wild with Hemingway*, page 32

Hemingway family history records that Ernest's first real gun was a single-barrel, single-shot 20-gauge shotgun (given to him by his grandfather Anson on his 10th birthday, 21 July 1909), but sometime in his teens he acquired a .22-caliber rifle and then a pistol, and thereafter seemingly was never without one or more of each. In addition to his various Colt Woodsman .22 pistols, we can point to at least six .22 rifles of Hemingway's—four pump-action models and a semiautomatic, all by Winchester, and one Marlin lever-action type. They appear in letters and narratives written by friends and relatives and by Ernest himself, and in photographs as well. They were go-to guns used for target practice and fun, hunting small game and dispatching wounded big game, and even home defense.

In July 1919, when he wrote to "Jenks and Barney" (Howell Jenkins and Lawrence Barnett) listing the guns he would have along on their camping trip in Michigan, Ernest advised them to bring "about 1000" .22 Long Rifle cartridges, "as they are cheap . . . and we will do a lot of shooting." [2] In 1919 a case lot of 1,000 rounds of .22LR cost about $10. The

*A Marlin lever-action Model 1897 made before 1917, with a 24-inch octagonal barrel and the standard-length magazine tube. Loosening the knurled knob on the side of the action allowed the rifle to be disassembled quickly for cleaning or transport. Hemingway's first .22 rifle, which he traded to his father when he was a 22-year-old newlywed, resembled this. An updated version of this rifle, called the Model 39A, is still in production.* Rock Island Auction Company

*David and Goliath. A .577 Nitro Express bullet—750 grains, nearly two ounces—dwarfs an entire .22 Long Rifle cartridge, with its tiny 40-grain bullet. Striking energy is a function of mass times velocity: The .22 bullet, emerging from the muzzle of a rifle at some 1,280 feet per second, delivers about 140 foot-pounds of energy; the striking energy of the colossal .577 slug, launched at just over 2,000 feet per second, is almost 50 times as much—6,600 foot-pounds.*

Steve Helsley

same thing can be had today for as little as $60. That was and is the key to the .22-caliber's tremendous popularity—even boys with just odd-job wages could afford to shoot .22s until they became marksmen. As noted in the previous chapter, in longevity and shots fired, no cartridge has ever rivaled the .22 rimfire, which was brought to market in 1857 as the .22 Short by Smith & Wesson for its first revolver.

In May 1930, during their exchange of letters about ordering the .30-06 Springfield from Griffin & Howe, Hemingway confided to Milford Baker, "I've never shot [any rifle] except a .22 cal. Marlin—and a .30-30 Winchester hunting."[3] The Winchester is never mentioned again; at the time it was an extremely popular deer rifle and may have been borrowed from a friend or his father. It would have been a lever-action, similar to the Marlin that Hemingway mentioned. This was the first successful lever-action rifle for the .22 cartridge, manufactured by the Marlin Firearms Company of New Haven, Connecticut. It debuted as the Model 1891, which begat Models 1892 and 1897, which became the Model 39 in 1921 and then the 39A in 1937; the changes in design from one to the next were minor. The Model 39A is still manufactured and still made to a high standard. Total production since 1891 is estimated to be in the neighborhood of three million. The Marlin .22 could be disassembled by hand into two sections, for cleaning or transport; it ejected spent shells to the side instead of upward, so a telescopic sight could easily be mounted on it; and it was not only smooth-functioning but also inherently accurate. Because even a .22 Long Rifle cartridge is only an inch long, the movement needed to cycle the gun—open the action and withdraw the empty case while recocking the hammer, then close it as a fresh round is fed in—is correspondingly short, just a quick down-and-up flick of the finger lever. The magazine tube under the Marlin's standard 24-inch barrel could hold 15 LR cartridges and it could be emptied quickly. Shooting a Marlin Model 91 with a longer magazine, Annie Oakley once set a record of 25 bullets into one ragged hole in a target in just 27 seconds. Ernest's request for a thousand rounds of .22-caliber ammunition was not out of line for three lads armed with a Marlin lever gun and a semi-automatic pistol and bent on fun.

In rural America, .22s were meant to teach youngsters more than just the fundamentals of accurate shooting; even a starter rifle brings with it significant responsibilities involving safety, respect for game and property laws, and maintenance. Learning these things often

nest stowed the illegal bird in the bottom of his boat, where, naturally, the game warden's son happened to spot it. A thoughtless, spur-of-the-moment lark spun out of control into flight from the law, confrontations with wardens and his parents, being hauled before a judge, a $15 fine and endless recrimination.

Another lesson came late, when Ernest was already 22 years old and had just married Hadley Richardson. In exchange for his father's settling some of his outstanding bills, Ernest gave him the little rifle. Leicester Hemingway recalled, "But then Father examined

*A pump-action .22-caliber Winchester Model 61 identical to Hemingway's rifle No. 203648. The standard model could fire Short, Long and Long Rifle ammunition interchangeably; the magazine tube under the 24-inch barrel held 14 Long Rifle cartridges, the most popular size. The take-down thumbscrew is on the left side of the action. Production began in 1932 and ended in 1963.*    James D. Julia Auctioneers

comes with some adolescent trauma. When he was 16, in July 1915, Ernest had a summer job on Michigan's Lake Walloon, where his family had a cottage, delivering the mail and selling vegetables from a small motorboat. As he told the story to his wife Mary, more than 30 years later, he was ferrying the Weyburn family up the lake when "a blue heron got up, the biggest I ever saw. I picked up my rifle, a .22-caliber Marlin, lever-action, and I thought, just for fun. Try to shoot him in the head . . . ." [4] Perversely, the difficult shot went home. Instead of abandoning the carcass, Er-

Ernest's Marlin .22 . . . . He turned to me, in a lesson-teaching mood. 'Look at this.' He held up the barrel of the dismantled rifle. 'This is the gun I taught Ernest to take care of properly. He let something get into the bore and then tried to shoot it out . . . . Now it will have to be completely rebored. Medals for military valor, but he ruins a good weapon like this.'" [5]

(In 1917 a Model 1897 Marlin with the standard 24-inch round barrel listed for $20.65; after the First World War the price jumped to $28.40, equivalent to $370 in 2010.)

*East Africa, October 1953. To the bemusement of these Masai, Papa takes aim at Earl Theisen's cigarette with a Winchester Model 61—not, however, No. 203648, which was made after this safari. Theisen, whom Papa nicknamed "Ty," was the photographer who spent a month covering the Hemingway safari for* Look *Magazine; he may have regretted handing his camera to Mary for this moment.*

John F. Kennedy Library

Whether by luck, instinct or common sense, Hemingway seems to have gotten through his teens and 20s without any memorable shooting accidents. Later, though, he should have shot the shark with his Woodsman while the fish was still in the water, which would have forestalled the ricochet that sent bullet fragments into his legs; and at least two mistakes led to the incident on the first safari, when one of Ernest's rifles—not only loaded and cocked but perhaps off-safety, too, as well as forgotten and not secured

in the rack—fell from the car roof and went off next to his head. The harrowing near-miss with Slim Hawks and her Browning A-5, in Idaho, was her fault, not Ernest's.

Despite such lapses in judgment, which could just as easily have ended in tragedy, there is ample evidence that Hemingway regarded .22s as somewhat less than awesomely lethal. Although he told *Esquire* readers that he could kill Gene Tunney or Joe Louis with a .22, he readily pointed .22s at friends holding cigarettes. Earl Theisen's moment, in

*Málaga, July 1959; the legendary 60th birthday party. Hemingway draws a bead on a cigarette in the lips of Antonio Ordóñez. Cooler heads were afraid that the bullet might go wide and hit Spain's greatest* torero. *These were not high-quality Winchester Gallery rifles but dilapidated, break-barrel single-shots. Among the champagne glasses, wine spills, loose ammunition, cigarettes and the lady's purse on the countertop is a second rifle, its barrel cranked open for loading. On the left, watching avidly, is Buck Lanham. As Col. Charles T. Lanham, he commanded the US 22nd Infantry Regiment in Normandy in 1944. Hemingway, covering WWII for* Collier's *Magazine, attached himself to Lanham for the battles of the Hürtgen Forest and the Bulge, and the two became great friends.*

A.E. Hotchner

Kenya, was captured on film by Mary Hemingway. Valerie Danby-Smith, the young freelance *Irish Times* reporter who became Ernest's secretary and then Valerie Hemingway when she married Ernest's youngest son Gregory, described even more risky business at Papa's 60th birthday party, in Málaga: "Mary rented a shooting gallery from a traveling carnival, and it became the main attraction when Ernest, to the horror and fascination of the onlookers, blasted the ash from Antonio's lighted cigarette with a .22 rifle as he held the butt between his lips." [6]

The Hemingways were in Spain so that Ernest could update *Death in the Afternoon,* his bullfighting masterpiece, and observe the increasingly deadly *mano-a-mano* duel of the two great *toreros*, the aging Luis Miguel Dominguín and the young Antonio Ordóñez, both his friends. To Ordóñez, who was recovering from being gored in the ring, a .22 bullet was perhaps of little account compared to a fighting bull. To top it off, Bhaiya, the Maharajah of Cooch Behar, then insisted that Hemingway shoot a cigarette from *his* lips too. (Don Ernesto's party, which required the attention of the fire department and broke up only at dawn the next day, passed into legend in Málaga.)

Hemingway did once fire a .22 at someone with intent: When the Finca Vigía was broken

less than 5 percent of a typical .30-06 round's, it is capable of real harm. Peter Hathaway Capstick, the professional hunter and safari author, wrote an apparently reliable account of two mature elephant bulls that were killed with single shots from a .22 rifle. In each case the bullet penetrated the thin skin behind the animal's foreleg and made its way to the heart, where it caused enough damage to lead, eventually, to death.

Twenty-two-caliber rifles were almost as popular in Europe as they were in America. A.E. Hotchner wrote of a road trip with Hemingway in the 1950s:

*An early Winchester Model 62 pump-action .22 rifle, distinguished from the Model 61 by its external hammer. Hemingway evidently owned at least two of this model as well; he had one in the 1940s and bought the second one from Abercrombie & Fitch in late 1959.*

James D. Julia Auctioneers

into for the third time, one night in January 1953, Ernest heard the intruders, got out of bed naked, and shot the last one as he was slipping out the bathroom window. The next morning, he and Mary followed the blood trail from the terrace outside the house down the hill. The consequences of killing a burglar could have been severe; two years earlier, the Hemingways' cook had accidentally shot himself in the shoulder with one of the household .22 rifles and Ernest was summoned to court to explain.

Although the energy of a .22LR bullet is

"We were motoring from Paris to Aix-en-Provence. It was normally a day's run, but it took us five. One of the things that slowed us was the fact that many of the little towns through which we passed had street fairs with shooting booths. These booths invariably offered as their most difficult target a cardboard pigeon that had a red eye about the size of a ball bearing. If the shooter, using a dilapidated .22, completely eradicated the red of the eye with three or four shots (depending on the generosity of the proprietor), he would win the booth's grand prize, a bottle of champagne.

*Gigi aboard* Pilar *in the Caribbean, c. 1943. By all accounts Gregory, aka Gigi, Ernest's third and youngest son, had a natural talent with guns that was the envy of most grown men. Patrick recalled that with this Winchester Model 62 his little brother could hit flying fish on the wing. (If the rifle had a serial number greater than 98200, it was a Model 62A.)* John F. Kennedy Library

"We riddled a lot of cardboard pigeons during that trip . . . ."[7]

The Winchester Repeating Arms Company had made a .22-rimfire version of its best-selling Model 1873 lever-action "cowboy" rifle, but it was heavy and expensive. Winchester called in designer John M. Browning, who as usual came up with a solution: In 1888 he and his son Matt were awarded a patent for a slide-action, tubular-magazine repeating rifle that Winchester put into production, in three different versions of .22 rimfire, as the Model 1890. Colt, just up the turnpike in Hartford, Connecticut, had introduced its "Lightning" pump-action rifle, in calibers ranging from .22 Short up to .50-95 Express, in 1884. It handled well, but mechanically it was fragile, and Browning's design quickly eclipsed it and set the standard for function and reliability. (Colt would thereafter stay in the handgun business, at least under its own name, while Winchester made only long guns.) In one or another form, the Model 1890 remained in production until 1963. Evidently most of the various .22 rifles that Hemingway owned as an adult were versions of this Winchester.

Like their stablemates, the Models 1897 and 1912 pump-action shotguns, which they resembled, these were all slick-operating, fast-handling, high-quality guns—for all that they were low-powered "plinkers."

Winchester's first evolution of the Model 1890 appeared in 1906, and this became the first version that could shoot all three types of the most popular .22 ammunition—Short, Long and Long Rifle—interchangeably and could quickly be taken down into two sections by hand for cleaning or transport. These improvements spurred sales and thereafter Winchester was careful always to offer these features in its standard-grade pump-action .22s. In 1932, when the 1890 and 1906 had each achieved sales of nearly a million units, the rifle was slightly re-engineered again and reintroduced in two versions, now called the Model 61 and the Model 62. The 61 was a modern hammerless gun—the hammer that struck the cartridge primer was hidden within the action—while the 62 stayed with the older, exposed-hammer design. In their drive across France, obliterating paper pigeon targets, Hotchner and Hemingway may have encountered a version of the M62 known as the Gallery rifle. This was made specifically for carnival shooting galleries; it was chambered for .22 Short only and had a special loading port. As well, the attendant could see at a glance if the hammer was cocked and he could make the gun safe—de-cock it—by lowering the hammer with his thumb instead of working the entire action.

By 1953, when the photo of Heming-way bedeviling Theisen was taken, the Winchester M61 had already been in production for 21 years; by the time manufacture ceased, 10 years later, more than 342,000 61s had been sold. The retail price was always low, especially for such a well-made rifle. On its debut, in 1932, the basic model cost $24.20 and by 1956 the price had climbed, just slightly ahead of inflation, to $55.15. By contrast, Colt's Woodsman .22 pistol then cost about $70. Since it was an entry-level gun as well as a knockabout for camp use, Winchester may have held down the price of the Model 61 to help bring customers into the fold at an early age. Then too, it was in 1963 that Winchester "discovered" it was losing money on so many of its guns and began to revamp its entire line; perhaps it was no coincidence that the overbuilt, under-priced M61 disappeared then.

Within a few years of swapping his Marlin lever-action .22 to his father, Ernest acquired his first Winchester Model 12, the superb pump shotgun he grew to rely on, so it's of little surprise that when the time came for another .22 rifle he sought out one from the same maker that was so similar mechanically. We have found no record of Hemingway's early purchase of a Model 61 or a Model 62, which of course were widely available and could have been bought anywhere, but it seems he eventually owned at least two of each.

In *Under Kilimanjaro* (258) he wrote of shooting eagles with a .22 Winchester during his bear hunting days in Wyoming or Montana in the 1930s. This is consistent with the

*Papa bought a semi-automatic Winchester Model 77 .22, Serial No. 99709, from Abercrombie & Fitch on 7 November 1959 for $53.95. Based on the photo of the gun rack in the following chapter, it was the tubular-magazine version and resembled this. Although he owned a number of Colt semi-auto .22 pistols and two Browning A-5 shotguns (as well as a number of WWII-souvenir pistols), Hemingway is on record as not favoring autoloaders.*

James D. Julia Auctioneers

debit date of 1932 for both the M61 and the M62. Much later, Mary learned to shoot with one or another of her husband's pump-action .22s—she called it an amusing toy, a bottle-shooting rifle—and in September 1953, on safari, she finished a wounded Thomson's gazelle with one of them, likely the M61 that Ernest used on Theisen's cigarette.

One of the guns that Mary consigned to Abercrombie & Fitch to sell after her husband's death was a Model 61. However, its serial number, 203648, dates its manufacture to mid-1954—*after* Ernest and Mary had returned from East Africa. (On 22 July 1963 A&F sold this rifle, with a full-length canvas case, to a man named Chester Booth for $45, $10 more than Hemingway's clapped-out Model 12 brought.) What became of the safari M61, which would have had a lower, earlier serial number? Did Papa also present it to Denis Zaphiro, with the Woodsman pistol? If Mary kept it for herself, where did it go after her death? Sean Larkin, the owner of Merkel No. 26724, also received from his father a Winchester Model 61 that may have been

part of Mary's bequest, but its serial number, 203843, dates it even later than the A&F consignment .22.

In the 1940s Hemingway had a Model 62, the external-hammer .22 rifle, that may have been kept aboard *Pilar*; we have found it in two photos, both taken on the boat in that time period, and Patrick Hemingway recalled that it had an octagonal barrel. No information about the origin or fate of this rifle has yet come to light, nor do we have a serial number.

However, there was at least one other Hemingway M62—No. 408404, made much later, in 1958, which he bought from Abercrombie & Fitch for $67.50 on 7 November 1959. (This was in fact a Model 62A, the evolution of the 62, which appeared in 1940 and was one of the last ever made.) On the same day he also bought a Winchester Model 77, a semi-automatic .22 rifle, Serial No. 99709, for $53.95. All of this is puzzling. Papa generally didn't care for "autos"; furthermore, he was 60 years old then, and his health was deteriorating rapidly.

# A THOMPSON SUBMACHINE GUN

*Tell Patrick I have a Thompson Sub Machine gun and we shoot sharks with it . . . As soon as they put their heads out we give them a burst.*

—to Sara Murphy, 10 July 1935, while Hemingway was in Bimini

Around noon on Sunday, 7 April 1935, Ernest Hemingway checked himself into the Marine Hospital in Key West to have bullet fragments removed from his legs. That morning, aboard *Pilar*, an attempt to dispatch a shark with his Woodsman .22 pistol had gone wrong. The fish, being dragged over the transom roller, thrashed and broke the gaff. Hemingway's bullet missed the shark's brain and instead hit a strip of railing, breaking apart and ricocheting back at him. The wounds were bloody but not severe. After a week to heal, Hemingway and his crew and guests (Charles Thompson and John and Katy Dos Passos) took *Pilar* across the Gulf Stream to Bimini. Big-game fishermen used the island as a base from which to troll for giant marlin and bluefin tuna. One day in early May, having not yet caught a tuna, Hemingway shifted from *Pilar* to a boat belonging to Charles Cook, manager of the fishing club on nearby Cat Cay. Cook was hooked up to a tuna he could not manage; after hours of fighting it, he was exhausted and shaking and his hands were bleeding. Hemingway slid into the fish-

ing chair and took over the rod. Now it became a test of Ernest's theory of how to boat a huge fish quickly, before the sharks could gather and tear it apart.

It didn't work. The battle went on through a thunder squall and heavy rain and into the night, and it attracted another spectator boat besides *Pilar*: *Moana*, the enormous yacht belonging to Bill Leeds Jr., son of William Bateman Leeds, the "Tinplate King," and Princess Xenia Georgievna of Russia. As Hemingway finally lifted the tuna to the surface, Leeds ordered spotlights on *Moana* to be trained on the fish. There too, in the glare, were the first sharks. As they attacked, the night erupted with gunfire—Leeds had opened up on them with some sort of automatic rifle.

It wasn't deterrent enough, though. By the time Cook's crew could boat the tuna, only its head remained, 249 pounds of it. Cook went back to Cat Cay; Leeds invited Hemingway and the Dos Passos aboard his yacht to dry out and have a drink. Hemingway naturally wanted to see his machine gun. He admired it—either a Thompson Model 1921 or '28—

so much that Leeds gave it to him.

By then, thanks to its reputation and its distinctive silhouette, the "Tommy gun" was already a household word. It was the invention of Gen. John Tagliaferro Thompson, West Point '82, US Army (ret'd). The slaughter wreaked by Hiram Maxim's machine gun in the Great War had convinced him that what the Doughboys needed was not their long-range bolt-action Springfield rifles but a high-

National Firearms Act of 1934, there were no restrictions on the sale of full-automatic guns in America.) In 1922 the firm published a famous poster depicting a rancher in a 10-gallon hat and woolly chaps blasting a gang of mounted desperados with a Thompson. A historian later wrote, "A company that could fancy a cowboy mowing down bandits, or envision a householder pouring machine gun fire into his darkened dining-room in defense

*A Thompson Model 1921AC, with the detachable buttstock, front pistol grip and a Cutts Compensator (hence the "C"), made by the Auto-Ordnance Corporation. The barrel, with its radial cooling fins, is 10½ inches long and the Cutts, which helped reduce felt recoil and muzzle jump, adds two more inches. This 20-round box magazine allowed precision aimed fire from the shoulder; the 100-round drum magazine was so big that the shooter's extended arm wouldn't reach around it. (A 50-round drum magazine was also available.)* James D. Julia Auctioneers

ly portable and compact automatic weapon for arm's-length trench warfare. The US Army and Marines tested his gun in 1920 and '21. *Scientific American* called it "the most efficient man killer of any firearm yet produced," but the military wasn't interested.

Thompson's company, the Auto-Ordnance Corporation, turned instead to police departments and the general public. (Prior to the

of the family silver, might well have misjudged its markets . . . . And so it came to pass that the Thompson—manufactured in peacetime, sold on the commercial market—was, in a sense, a machine gun for the home." [1] In fact it sold much better to police departments than to homeowners, and it was not inexpensive. In the early 1920s the retail price was about $175, equivalent to $2,300 in 2010. Leeds' gift

Auto-Ordnance's famous 1922 Thompson poster: "a machine gun for the home."

to Hemingway was a valuable one.

To Gen. Thompson's dismay, one "commercial market" immediately embraced his product: criminals. The first recorded use of a Thompson in gang warfare was in Chicago on 25 September 1925. (With the gun's impressive staccato rattle, this led to the nickname "Chicago typewriter.") Within a decade Thompson's gun, with plenty of help from Hollywood, would be forever associated with bootleggers, Al Capone, "Machine Gun" Kelly, The St. Valentine's Day Massacre and J. Edgar Hoover's FBI. True success, however, had to wait till the next world war, when the Tommy gun proved ideal for house-to-house combat in Europe and uprooting Japanese forces dug into the Pacific Islands. It was still on duty with the American military as late as the Vietnam War.

Thompson coined the term "sub-machine gun" for his invention, meaning an automatic weapon that fires a pistol round. Nearly all production Thompsons were chambered for the .45 ACP cartridge, developed by John Browning and used in his Colt Model 1911 semi-auto military pistol. This was an inspired, if obvious, choice both logistically, for it reduced the variety of ammunition a soldier had to deal with, and ballistically—the fat 230-grain bullet hit hard. It was effective on many targets, including sharks, and Hemingway loved to shoot it. Auto-Ordnance had slowed the gun's rate of fire

*The Gulf Stream, c. 1935. Hemingway fires his Thompson submachine gun from a boat; note the empty shell cases in the air. It appears not to have a Cutts Compensator on its muzzle.*
John F. Kennedy Library

to about 880 rounds per minute and settled its weight at around 12 well-balanced pounds (with the various stick magazines), so keeping the muzzle on target was much easier than legend has it. In photos Hemingway, a precision rifleman, fires his Thompson from the shoulder, not the hip, and uses the sights instead of spraying it like a hose; he had a vested interest in keeping the fire away from his trophy fish. The key was to direct short, controlled bursts at the base of a shark's dorsal fin. The gun could be switched to fire single shots as well.

Along with being highly accurate and effective out to 100 yards, the Thompson was also well machined and extraordinarily simple, with few moving parts, and it could be disassembled for cleaning in less than two minutes

and without tools. All this made the weapon ideal not only for the battlefield but also for marine use. It is likely that Hemingway's Thompson was carefully hidden away aboard *Pilar*, although America's National Firearms Act would not have bothered him in Cuba.

In *Esquire*'s July 1935 issue, Hemingway wrote of using it to try to drive sharks away from a marlin he estimated at close to a ton. We have found no evidence of the Thompson after this, but it may still have been on *Pilar* (with all the military hardware and the Westley Richards .577 Nitro Express) during the anti-U-boat patrols in 1942 and '43. And it may have gone over the side in early 1958, when Ernest and Gregorio jettisoned *Pilar*'s hidden weaponry as Cuba's revolution heated up.

# A Big-Bore Mauser, or Two

*I am taking a 30.06—10.75 Mauser—12 ga shotgun (pump) and 6.5 Mannlicher—also my Colt 22 cal Woodsman*

—to Mike Strater, 9 February 1932, while Hemingway was at Key West

The one "big gun" in Hemingway's African writings, whether journalism, memoir or fiction, that is not a double-barreled rifle is a bolt-action .505 Gibbs. Hemingway armed his character Robert Wilson, the white hunter in "The Short Happy Life of Francis Macomber," with one—"shockingly big-bored"; a "damned cannon"—and wrote of "the unbelievable smash of the .505 with a muzzle velocity of two tons."

The Gibbs dates back to the very beginning of the still-ongoing debate between bolt-action and double-barreled rifles for dangerous game. In the late 19th Century, big-game hunters relied on single-shot or side-by-side doubles chambered for massive cartridges such as the 8-bore (.840 caliber), which fired a 1,250-grain bullet, and the 4-bore (1.04 caliber), with an 1,880-grain bullet. As pointed out in the Westley Richards chapter, these rifles were enormously heavy and difficult to shoot and, because of the sheer volume of blackpowder needed to get adequate power, their cartridges were too long and thick for use in bolt-action rifles. However, in 1884, a

Frenchman named Paul Vieille formulated *Poudre B*, the first practical form of high-energy smokeless powder. The consequences were far-reaching for both cartridge and gun design, not to say warfare and hunting.

In 1887, an exceptional London gunmaker (and marksman) named John Rigby was appointed superintendent of the Royal Enfield Rifle Factory and charged with shepherding the transition of Britain's service rifles from clumsy blackpowder single-shots to smokeless, magazine-fed, bolt-action repeaters such as the Mauser and Mannlicher. (Military use always came first.) The various bolt-action types, none terribly different, were being perfected; they could be relied on to feed and then fire a round accurately, extract and eject the empty case, and do this again, and again and again under battlefield conditions. Furthermore, their design would soon be completely industrialized for low-cost mass production.

When John Rigby left government service and resumed his role as head of J. Rigby & Co., in 1894, he had not only a firm grasp on the latest in repeating-rifle technology and bullet construction, but also a particular appreciation for the German battle rifle. He struck a deal with Mauser-Werke, in Oberndorf, to be its distributor for the United Kingdom and the British Colonies. But he went far beyond simply selling commercial Mausers. It is partly through his efforts that Paul Mauser joined Oliver Winchester, Samuel Colt, Pietro Beretta and Mikhail Kalashnikov as gunmakers of global significance.

Cartridge cases for the first generations of smokeless-powder military ammunition were

new round, just under 3¾ inches overall, fired a superbly designed 410-grain bullet at 2,400 feet per second with a muzzle energy of 5,100 foot-pounds. It proved extremely effective on even the largest animals, and for the first time a bolt-action repeating rifle could compete on an even footing with the heavy doubles. Big-game hunters took to it immediately and the .416 Rigby is still very popular in Africa.

(Late in his 1930 correspondence about hunting rifles with Milford Baker, which led him to buy the Springfield .30-06 and then

*A handsome .505 Gibbs built by Griffin & Howe on a Magnum bolt action supplied by Mauser, in Oberndorf, Germany, and given Serial No. 1015 (and engraved initials "MS"). Hemingway's Mauser-based .505, numbered 1691 by Griffin & Howe, probably resembled this right down to the Lyman aperture rear sight, which he also had on his G&H Springfield, and the thick recoil pad and other features.* James D. Julia Auctioneers

generally less than 2½ inches long and held no more than 60 grains of powder—a charge that was effective against even distant human targets but couldn't produce enough force to reliably kill elephant, Cape buffalo, rhino and the like. John Rigby convinced Mauser to lengthen its Model 1898 rifle action to accept longer, more powerful cartridges. The resultant Magnum Mauser action would have a tremendous impact, literally and figuratively, on big-game hunting. Around 1911 Rigby introduced the first cartridge designed for the Magnum action: the .416 Rigby. The

his first Mannlicher-Schoenauer, Hemingway indicated he might buy a ".416 Magnum Mauser" if he could get it at a good price, but there is no A&F/G&H record of such a purchase.[1])

The .505 Rimless Magnum—as it was originally dubbed—was brought to market almost at the same time by George Gibbs, a gunmaker in Bristol, England, whose name soon became attached to his creation. (Gibbs may have caught wind of Rigby's .416 and decided to one-up his competitor.) It too was conceived for the Magnum Mauser action, and Mauser's records indicate that the factory in Oberndorf built its own first .416 and .505 rifles in the same year, 1912. Gibbs's .505 is still the biggest standard repeating-rifle caliber, at least in diameter, and it is still somewhat shocking to behold a rifle barrel with a bore diameter more akin to a 28-gauge shotgun. Hemingway was mixing up his ballistics when he wrote of "muzzle velocity of two tons"—velocity is measured in feet per second—but he made his point: It is almost gratuitously powerful. Five-oh-five ammunition was first available with 525- or 535-grain bullets, which deliver some 6,200 foot-pounds of energy at the muzzle of the gun. *Three* tons.

The Short Happy Life of Francis Macomber" debuted in the September 1936 issue of *Cosmopolitan* Magazine and it has been entertaining readers and winding up academics ever since. It is probably based on a 1908 safari scandal that involved John H. Patterson, killer of the man-eating lions of Tsavo, and affected Blayney Percival, the older brother of Philip Percival, Hemingway's "Pop" character. It is easy to imagine Percival telling the tale to his client Hemingway one evening around the campfire on their 1933 safari. Hemingway chose knowingly in arming his fictional Wilson, a direct and somewhat brutal man, with such a formidable weapon.

Equally interesting is that years after his first safari—and even more years before his second one—Hemingway bought a .505 for himself. Naturally, there are questions.

Page 359 of the Griffin & Howe sales ledgers seems clear: On 18 February 1941 Ernest Hemingway ordered a .505 Gibbs, G&H Serial No. 1691, built on a Mauser Magnum bolt action with a 26-inch barrel, weighing 9 pounds 9 ounces. On 29 May 1941 Hemingway's account was charged $275 for the finished rifle.

Also clear, however, is that on 31 January '41 Ernest and Martha had boarded the SS *Matsona* in San Francisco to sail to Hawaii and on to Hong Kong and then travel overland to the Canton Front to cover the Sino-Japanese War for *PM* and *Collier's*. On February 14 they were hosted at a party in Chungking, in southwestern China, and by February 18 Ernest was in Rangoon, Burma—halfway around the world from New York. (Martha had gone on to Java and then Singapore.) On April 29 Hemingway was in Hong Kong again and on May 19 he arrived back in San Francisco after a grueling 12-day trip by flying boat. Ernest and Martha were reunited in late May in Washington, DC, and spent the first two weeks of June in New York before returning home to Cuba.

Picking up the Mauser at Abercrombie & Fitch was possible on May 29, but how did Ernest place the order for it on February 18? By mail? By telegram from Rangoon? It would be more likely that Abercrombie's ordered the rifle from G&H (its subsidiary) for inventory and that Hemingway spotted it in the rack at A&F on May 29 and bought it on impulse, perhaps as a reward for himself after the long and difficult China assignment. (He would do this four years later, upon his return to New York from the European theater of WWII—

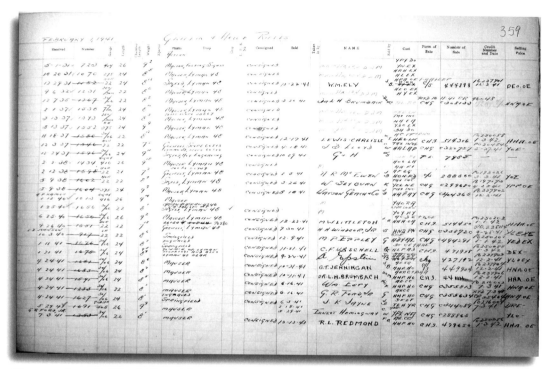

*The page from Griffin & Howe's ledgers that records—it's the second listing from the bottom—the 1941 order and pickup of Ernest Hemingway's .505. Note the absence of the word "consigned." Prices are in G&H's internal letter code. (The client two lines higher, by the way, is not the Gerald R. Ford who became the 28th president of the United States.)*  Griffin & Howe

walk into A&F and snap up the pair of Brokaw Merkels.) But such a gun is clearly marked in the ledger, in red ink, as "consigned."

In any event, a .505 has no utility anywhere but in Africa, and Hemingway would not go on safari again until 1953. And when he did, he brought along his double-barreled Westley Richards .577 Nitro Express, an even more powerful rifle. What became of the big Mauser? Its serial number, 1691, comes from Griffin & Howe; Mauser would have applied

its own, much higher number to the action. Mauser authority Jon Speed, author of *Oberndorf Sporting Rifles*, has found only one Mauser in caliber .505 Gibbs that was shipped to G&H before the Second World War: No. 105459, in 1931. However, this was a completed rifle sold under the Mauser name, while Hemingway's .505 was nominally a Griffin & Howe built on a Mauser action and thus re-numbered by G&H. At the time, Mauser components supplied to American gunmakers such as G&H,

Hoffmann Arms and others were imported by the Stoeger company of New York City.

And what of the lighter Mauser that Ernest intended to bring to East Africa on his first safari, the 10.75mm he referred to in the letter at the top of this chapter? Two months earlier, in December 1931, he had written to Strater about a "10.5 Mauser" that a friend loaned him, the friend saying that it was good for buffalo but a little small for elephant. There is no nominal 10.5mm big-game cartridge; Hemingway meant 10.75.

There were two such rounds at the time. Hemingway probably was referring to the German version, the 10.75x68mm, which was introduced by Mauser around 1908 and then began to fade from view during the 1940s. Its 347-grain bullet generated 3,700 foot-pounds of energy at the rifle muzzle, which put it on the threshold of the dangerous-game class. However, it earned a bad reputation among some African professionals because its bullets, both the soft-nose and the solid, broke up too easily on impact (instead of penetrating). John Taylor, the Irish ivory hunter who tested and wrote extensively about big-game cartridges in the 1930s and '40s, pooh-poohed the commercial Mauser 10.75x68 as a "cheap, mass-production rifle that once flooded Africa"[2] and was popular among hunters who wouldn't or couldn't buy proper equipment. In other words, Hemingway's friend had it right—acceptable on buffalo, too light for elephant.

The other 10.75, in a case 73mm (2.87 inches) long, was better known, at least in the English-speaking world, as the .404 Jeffery. Few hunters ever complained about this one or died because it failed them in a bad spot. It is only about 10 percent more powerful than the 68mm German round, but its bullets are slightly heavier and perform much better. William J. Jeffery was a contemporary of Rigby and Gibbs who set up shop in London in 1888. He too seized upon the Mauser action, although not the Magnum version, as a way to provide double-rifle power in a much less expensive, single-barrel repeater. His .404 Rimless Nitro Express (inexplicably, the actual bullet diameter is 0.423 inches—10.75mm) appeared around 1905, meant to duplicate the performance of the medium-weight .450/400 Nitro double-rifle cartridge. When they appeared a few years later, the .416 and .505 substantially outperformed it.

Hemingway's February '32 letter to Mike Strater[3] was written almost 21 months before he arrived in Kenya for his first safari. At that point, with Pauline's wealthy "Uncle Gus" Pfeiffer's promise to pay for the trip burning a hole in his pocket, he had already been trying to put the expedition together since at least May of 1930. Planning for such an adventure can be nearly as absorbing as actually carrying it out, and Hemingway delighted in reading everything about African hunting that he could get his hands on and then disseminating advice to the friends he'd invited along—Charles Thompson from Key West and two fellow expats he'd befriended in Paris in the '20s: painter Henry (Mike) Strater and poet Archie MacLeish. The rest of that letter discusses everything from sleeping bags to safari prices and how best to get to Africa.

One thing or another kept interfering and Ernest didn't get to Africa until December 1933—and then only with Thompson and Pauline. Based on his friend's advice, Hemingway may have taken the loaned Mauser "10.5" along to fill the gap between his Springfield .30-06 and the "double express rifles (2nd hand)" he expected to buy or rent in Nairobi. We have no evidence that he bought a 10.75 before the trip—they were available, if exceedingly rare, in America—or even that such a rifle was in camp on that safari. If he showed up with his friend's loaned Mauser, the veteran Percival may simply have talked him out of using it.

Had Hemingway meant the other 10.75, the 73mm version, it seems likely he would have referred to it as the .404 Jeffery instead.

# THE W. & C. SCOTT & SON PIGEON GUN

*. . . a straight-stocked long-barreled Scott live-pigeon full choke in both barrels that I had bought from a lot of shotguns a dealer had brought down from Udine to the Kechlers' villa in Codroipo.* —Under Kilimanjaro, *page 392*

No serious wingshooter—and Papa was, first and last, a serious and perhaps even brilliant wingshot—can go for long without at least contemplating pigeon shooting. Hemingway apparently was introduced to the sport in France early in the 1930s by Ben Gallagher ("The Browning Superposed") and later became a top scorer in the pigeon ring at the Club des Cazadores del Cerro, in Cuba.

Shooting boxed pigeons is akin to one of Hemingway's other passions, bullfighting—although the gunner hardly shares the risk of the *torero.* While enemies of the blood sports see only a human practicing slaughter for personal aggrandizement, aficionados appreciate that the person behind the gun or the *muleta* seeks to demonstrate the most awesome skill of all: the ability to deal death personally and artistically. Whether they are city-park birds or distinct species such as the blue rock or the band-tail, pigeons are strong, agile and fast, heavily muscled and broad-winged. To bring down an escaping, evading pigeon at a distance takes reflexive skill; to do it consis-

*A well-worn W. & C. Scott & Son Monte Carlo B—Serial No. 60293, c. 1898, with 30-inch Damascus (twist-forged) barrels and a stock extension with a soft recoil pad. Note the round cocking-indicator window in the lockplate. Appropriately for a pigeon gun, it has a non-automatic safety catch, double triggers and two ivory sighting beads on its rib. The Monte Carlo B also has a Greener-style "treble-grip" locking crossbolt. Lloyd Arnold described Hemingway's Scott as "a plain piece, but handsome in its clean lines."*

Rob Shelton/Steve Helsley

tently in a long-running match requires great concentration and more than a bit of good luck. Along with high, fast British-style driven gamebirds, boxed pigeons are the toughest test of a shotgunner.

Competitive live-pigeon shooting began in England in the late 1700s. By 1812, when the first pigeon-shooting club, the Old Hats Tavern, was established in London, rules regarding scoring, distances, shooting styles, guns and cartridges were being formalized. Other clubs quickly sprang up—the Old Hornsey Wood House, Red House, Battersea, the Gun Club and many more—and the sport spread across Britain and then to France, Spain, Italy and onward. It became a phenomenon of the wealthy and influential where entry fees, prize money and side wagers eventually mounted into the thousands. It also became a proving ground for makers who chose to put their guns and ammunition into the hands of top shooters for all to witness their performance. The sporting press followed these contests closely, reporting the outcomes—and the inevitable disagreements, penalties, scandals and disgraces—to followers everywhere.

The pigeon shot stands at the hub of an arc of five or seven "traps"—boxes five yards apart and up to 31 yards from the gun. Twenty or more yards beyond the semi-circle of traps is the penalty line, the fence inside which a pigeon must fall in order to be scored. The shooter calls for a bird; at random, one or another of the boxes spring open and the pigeon inside is released. A live bird accelerating off the ground at unpredictable angles and flying

*Torcello, Italy, fall 1948. Hemingway shows off his newly acquired Scott gun while setting out with one of Count Kechler's or Baron Franchetti's gamekeepers to hunt ducks. Note the decoys in the bow of the boat. Torcello is an island in the Lagoon of Venice, a few miles northeast of the city.* John F. Kennedy Library

*Cuba, late spring 1952. The Finca Vigía had been plagued by a series of break-ins. Hemingway and his 12-gauge Scott were on guard. One night in January '53 thieves entered the house again. Ernest heard them, slipped out of bed, picked up a .22 rifle and fired a shot at the last one escaping out this bathroom window. Mary wrote that the next morning they found blood on the terrace outside.* John F. Kennedy Library

American event took place at the Sportsman's Club of Cincinnati. As it had in England, "trap shooting" spread rapidly. A famously ballyhooed competition in Louisville, Kentucky, in 1883 pitted professional sharpshooter and showman William F. "Doc" Carver against Capt. A.H.—Adam Henry—Bogardus, the American and world pigeon champion. (Carver outshot the captain 19 times in 25 matches.) By this time, pigeon tournaments in America were drawing huge crowds and making celebrities of their stars.

Pigeon shooting reached its zenith with a one-time appearance at the Olympics, in the Paris games of 1900, where the top four guns agreed to split the 20,000-franc first prize. But, especially in America and England, public antipathy toward using live targets had been building for decades and thereafter competitive wingshooting changed dramatically. Already in the 1860s, then driven largely by the spiraling cost of live pigeons, inventors were experimenting with fragile glass balls (sometimes filled with feathers) and catapults; then in 1880 came the "clay pigeon" as we know it today—a molded disk launched by a spring-loaded "trap." All manner of shotgun

fast and erratically made the sport challenging for the gun, but outsize prizes and personalities, not to say betting, made it addictive even for spectators.

Live pigeon shooting had crossed the Atlantic by 1831, when the first recorded

*Wingshooting in Kenya, the second safari: Hemingway with his Scott, possibly pass-shooting sand grouse or doves by a water hole somewhere in the open country north of their Kimana camp—a kind of game shooting for which a pigeon gun is well suited. Note the forward sling swivel, which was removed by A&F in 1960. Denis Zaphiro is backing Papa up. Both men have bolt-action rifles handy, just in case. On the skyline behind Zaphiro is Mawenzi, the Kilimanjaro Massif's second-most easterly peak. The main peak, Kibo, swathed in cloud, lies behind Hemingway.*

John F. Kennedy Library

games with inanimate targets have been devised since, but the sport of pigeon shooting still exists, mostly in Spain and parts of Latin America and in some private US gun clubs.

In 1931 Hemingway wrote to his friend Mike Strater that he'd been shooting live pigeons in Kansas City ("fly like hell") and that a big match was coming up, with an entry fee of $120 and $2,500 in prize money. His average, he wrote, was 20 birds out of 30, and he added that pigeon shooting was available only in Pennsylvania, Missouri and Kentucky.[1]

A decade later, there were no restrictions in Cuba, where the Club des Cazadores served the same purpose as a country club does today, with shotguns in lieu of golf clubs. Shooting there became a Hemingway family activity. The local press, Papa bragged, reported that no other four guns in Cuba could outshoot him and his three sons in the pigeon ring. Jack, the eldest Hemingway son, wrote that the best of them was Gigi: "He used his little single-shot .410 to deadly effect and the following winter [1941] would be runner-up in the World Live Pigeon Shooting Championship, which was held in Havana that year because of the war in Europe. He was a natural. At age eleven he did not feel the pressure of the competition as severely as others."[2] For a small boy with a very light single-shot gun to beat adult champions armed with bespoke 12-gauges is a remarkable feat.

Early in 1946, Mary Hemingway wrote: "on a bright, windy afternoon I went along with Ernest to the Club de Cazadores, pleasantly old-fashioned under its towering laurel trees. He had got a shipment of *correos*, strong, fast-flying pigeons, down from the north and had organized a private shoot with some friends.

"Ernest gallantly chose me for his team and I discovered that day that pigeon shooting as a participating game was vastly more entertaining than it was as a spectacle. We had twenty pigeons apiece to shoot and each time I walked out the cement path to call '*Listo*' and then '*pajarero*' my breath faded away. Most of the time after I had shot my two barrels, my hope faded away too. My total score was nine birds knocked down inside the fence. But Ernest had a near perfect score."[3]

Photographs before 1948 show Papa shooting pigeons at the club with a Browning Superposed or his long-barreled, Full-choke Model 12 Winchester. Lloyd Arnold wrote that Hemingway's Superposed (the gun he won from Ben Gallagher in France in the early '30s) had relatively short, open-choke barrels, which would hardly have been ideal for pigeons. A competition pigeon gun, on which a score worth thousands of dollars might hang, is typically long-barreled but neutrally balanced, to swing smoothly yet respond quickly to changes in the bird's direction. Both barrels would be choked for long-range effect. Its buttstock is quite straight, to help absorb recoil and to throw shot slightly high, for a rising bird. Pigeon guns are heavier than conventional game guns, also to absorb recoil and because more powerful competition cartridges require a stouter frame and action. Like a rifle built for big game, a pigeon gun must be as foolproof as possible; some even have no safety catch, which might conceivably interfere with a shot.

The pressure of live-pigeon competition did much to advance the technology of the shotgun and its ammunition, and virtually every maker whose products won pigeon tournaments could be relied on to boast of this in its advertising. The English firm of W. & C. Scott & Son especially embraced pigeon shooting, a fact of which Ernest Hemingway surely was aware. A company history records more than 100 wins or outstanding performances in "publicly recorded matches" with Scott guns between 1873 and 1913 in London, Monte Carlo, Paris, Naples, Seville, Munich and other European venues and from Melbourne, Australia, to New York to Los Angeles and back to Worcester, Massachusetts. Of course guns alone do not win trophies, and Scott wooed many champions. Captain Bogardus won six major competitions with Scott guns between 1878 and 1887 in America alone.

*Hemingway cradling his Scott gun, the action open and its Greener-style locking extension clearly visible. The snowcapped summit of Mt. Kilimanjaro, at 19,341 feet the tallest mountain on the African continent, has emerged from the clouds.* John F. Kennedy Library

With the advent of the self-contained cartridge and the break-action, breechloading double-barreled gun, circa 1860, innumerable mechanisms were patented—in the USA, the United Kingdom and Continental Europe—to open and close gun barrels. What became accepted, the global standard that continues in production to this day, was a combination of three designs developed by gunmakers in the UK: the Westley Richards toplever, patented in 1858, which is pushed by the shooter's thumb; the Purdey underbolt (1863), which slides horizontally into notches under the barrels, to lock the gun closed; and the vertical spindle that passes through the rear of the action body to connect the two, which was patented by William Middleditch Scott in 1865.

Together with Anson & Deeley's 1875 firing mechanism, as described in "The .577 Nitro Express," and several other seminal designs and styles, these made the modern double-barreled gun or rifle an entirely British affair.

William Middleditch Scott was the elder son of William Scott, who with his brother Charles established the gunmaking firm of W. & C. Scott in 1840. Like William Westley Richards before him, William Scott had settled in Birmingham, already the capital city of England's industrial midlands, where talented craftsmen could find work and sometimes even make their fortunes. The company became W. & C. Scott & Son when William Middleditch joined, probably in the 1850s. His younger brother James Charles followed him into the business, but "Son" never became plural. Perhaps this is because it was William Middleditch who left the greater mark, not only on the Scott family firm but also on gunmaking in general. The Scott spindle and its thumb lever, mounted atop the "wrist" of the stock at the rear of the action, made opening the gun a simple and efficient movement, one

that did not require the shooter to change his grip (as almost all others did). William Middleditch was awarded many gunmaking patents, but this was his crowning achievement and because of it the Scott name has outlived the company itself.

If the "quality" of the British gun trade was in London, the "quantity" was in Birmingham. Most of the vast numbers of military, export and trade guns that the British Empire required were made in Birmingham. For that matter, however, many London guns began as component parts or even entire unfinished guns in Birmingham. By the 1860s W. & C. Scott & Son was supplying both ends (and the middle) of the gun business and contributing significantly to the hundreds of thousands of firearms being shipped from the UK to the American Civil War. The company prospered and grew. After building a larger factory, Scott opened retail shops in London and Turin, and then bought Moore & Harris, a lesser Birmingham gunmaker, in order to get its distribution system in the United States.

W. & C. Scott & Son probably became even better known overseas than at home. In England, Scott made guns that were generally retailed under others' names, while in Europe by 1890 the company held royal commissions with the Kings of Spain, Norway and Sweden, and in the US Scott dealers were spread from San Francisco to Boston. The 1884 price list for the E.C. Meacham Arms Co., Saint Louis, Missouri, offered a wide range of Scott guns, hammer and hammerless, priced from $83.12 to $300—the same price as a top-of-the-line

*Wingshooting on safari. Still only 54, Papa shows the wear and tear of a rugged, high-mileage, hard-drinking and accident-prone life (although the worst was yet to come). This is the best photo of the long-barreled and straight-stocked Scott gun.*

John F. Kennedy Library

Parker, the highest-quality shotgun then produced in the United States.

Scott made its name in America not only by winning pigeon tournaments but also by earning prizes for design innovation at industrial exhibitions in Philadelphia (1876), Boston (1883), Chicago (1893) and St. Louis (1904). At the time, veteran shooters were suspicious of the new breed of hammerless guns because they could not tell if the gun was cocked by glancing at the external hammers. Scott's trademark "crystal cocking indicators" were small portholes covered with glass in the sideplates of the action that let the shooter see whether the tumblers (the internal hammers) were in the cocked position. Also appreciated in America, where a gunsmith might be far away, was a simple adjustment on Scott guns that could compensate for wear in the hinge joint from heavy use.

In October 1897 Scott merged with P. Webley & Son to form Webley & Scott Revolver and Arms Co., Ltd., shortened to Webley & Scott in 1906. After the First World War, which, as the saying went, "killed half its gunmakers and a third of their clients," Britain's gun trade went into decline and many of its hundreds of companies disappeared. W. & C. Scott & Son was more fortunate. While it endured a bewildering series of consolidations, closures and re-openings, for the next 80 years, with interruptions for war production, Webley & Scott was the largest manufacturer of double guns in England, at its peak employing 2,000 workers. As before, most of these guns were finished and sold by other companies—Hol-

land & Holland, William Evans, Grant & Lang and more. In 1979 W&S ceased production of double guns. A year later, W. & C. Scott was re-formed and began to build mid- and high-priced double guns under its own name again—an effort that lasted until 1991, when death became final.

Some guns, of course, were always made and sold under the Scott name, and Hemingway's was one of these—a Monte Carlo B, a model that was introduced in 1891 as competitive pigeon shooting was approaching its zenith. Although the "B" implies a second-grade gun, there was no Monte Carlo "A" (and the B was itself available in two grades, or levels of finish). Crawford and Whatley, in *The History of W. & C. Scott Gunmakers*, described the Monte Carlo B as the firm's most popular sidelock shotgun, adding that it "was a great favorite of competition shooters and often was made as a pigeon gun, although game and wildfowl [waterfowl] versions were available." It was offered in gauges ranging from 10 to 28, although pigeon guns were virtually always 12-bores, and it had the locking cross-bolt invented by W.W. Greener, another English gunmaker. Even after the company name changed to Webley & Scott, the Monte Carlo B was always marked "W. & C. Scott & Son." Although far less costly than a best-grade London gun from Purdey or Boss, it was hardly inexpensive. In its final year of production, 1935, it had a retail price of £35—five months' pay for a farm or factory laborer. In total, only some 2,000 were built, an infinitesimal frac-

*Idaho, late 1950s, at the private cabin that Hemingway and friends called the Silver Creek Rod & Gun Club. Papa hand-launches a magpie for a guest. The birds were considered such pests that Idaho put a 5¢ bounty on them and ranch boys trapped them for pocket money. Hemingway, intrigued by the bird's erratic flight and cunning, devised his own local form of "pigeon" shooting, complete with rules, trophies and wagering. Mary Hemingway wrote fondly of their magpie shoots—the friends and food and wine, the wind that made the targets so difficult, and the parceling out of the betting pool. This was much more relaxed than the high-pressure pigeon matches of Cuba and Europe where Hemingway had become a master.* John F. Kennedy Library

tion of the company's total output.

In Italy in the autumn of 1948, while Ernest was working on *Across the River and Into the Trees*, he and Mary stayed with Count Carlo Kechler and his family at their villa in Codroipo, northeast of Venice. As the epigraph at the top of this chapter indicates, this was when he acquired his Scott, possibly secondhand. Lloyd Arnold attributed the gun to a "marketing firm" called Angelini & Bernardon [4], which in fact was an importer of guns and hunting gear (now defunct) in Trieste. If A&B was a regular customer of W. & C. Scott, Scott may have stamped or engraved the company's name on the gun, where Arnold would have seen it. Evidently Papa did not buy the gun from Angelini & Bernardon, but from a dealer in Udine, halfway between Trieste and Codroipo. It seems he put it to use right away, taking it duck hunting in the quiet waters of the lagoon that surrounds Venice, where a windblown piece of wadding from a cartridge lodged in his eye and caused an infection. Thereafter the Scott saw use elsewhere in Europe, at the pigeon club in Cuba, and in East Africa on the 1953-'54 safari.

A degree of mystery attaches to it, however. Lloyd Arnold: "For some reason or other he reached into his literary character file and called it the 'Adams gun' and said he liked it as well as any he had ever owned." [4] Why Adams? There is more mystery, too.

Ironically, until now one of the *least* known things about Papa's guns is which one ended his life, on 2 July 1961, at his home in Ketchum, Idaho. However, we believe we have the answer.

At least one police officer at the time told the press it was an over/under. Some people assume it was his beloved Model 12. Russia's Охотаи Рыбалка (*Hunting & Fishing*) Magazine recently speculated that the suicide gun was a Bernardelli. *Life* Magazine simply reported it was a double-barreled shotgun. However, the Wikipedia entry is typical of what is widely accepted: "Hemingway is believed to have purchased the Boss & Co. shotgun he used to commit suicide through Abercrombie & Fitch." Some accounts are so detailed as to add that an A&F salesman named Charlie Wicks sold Papa the gun. Thus, through the A&F ledgers, identifying such a Boss—a rare and expensive gun—should be relatively easy.

While historian Bob Beach was searching the Abercrombie & Fitch records, author Calabi was reading the Hemingway literature for Boss mentions. There is one: In *Across the River and Into the Trees* the hero daydreams about the guns he might get for the woman he loves, if they ever go hunting together—"a good Purdey 12, not too damn light, or a pair of Boss over-and-unders."

Author Sanger, meanwhile, was on the ground in Idaho. Soon after Hemingway's death, the gun that he had turned on himself was handed over to a welder in Ketchum to be destroyed. The stock was smashed and the steel parts cut up with a torch. The mangled remnants were then buried in a field. Michael DeChevrieux, a gun collector in Hailey, Idaho, mentioned to Sanger that some of these pieces

*The key to the puzzle—the remnant scrap of left lockplate, less than three-quarters of an inch long, its burnt edge showing the effects of an oxy-acetylene torch.* Steve Helsley

might still exist. Sanger visited the welding shop, which is still in business. The proprietor is the grandson of the man who destroyed the gun in 1961; he inherited the shop from his father—who still had a few of the gun's pieces in a matchbox. The remnant scraps amount to three bits of shattered stockwood, portions of the two triggers, part of a barrel lump and a small chunk of a left lockplate.

Sanger photographed the pieces, and the authors' immediate reaction—*This is no Boss!*—was borne out by expert opinion from English gunmaker David Trevallion. Among other things, the screw on the lockplate that holds the intercepting-sear spring is in the wrong place. So it was not a Boss; but what was it? DeChevrieux examined the tiny bit of lock and proclaimed the distinctive border engraving on the plate to be that of a W. & C. Scott & Son Monte Carlo B.

*Border-engraving detail from the destroyed Hemingway lockplate.*
Steve Helsley

*Border-engraving detail from a lockplate of Monte Carlo B No. 60293.*
Steve Helsley

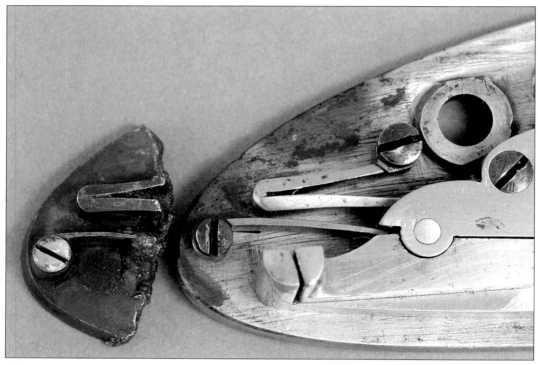

*The piece of destroyed lockplate with the corresponding lock from the Shelton Monte Carlo B, Serial No. 60293. The minor differences, in spring thickness and screws, can be attributed to a difference in age, and thus production, between the two guns.*

Steve Helsley

Another collector, Rob Shelton, offered a Monte Carlo B (Serial No. 60293, the gun shown here) for comparison, and the Hemingway scraps were loaned to the authors for closer evaluation. Comparing the left sidelock from Shelton's Scott to the piece provided by the retired welder leads to an inescapable conclusion. Forrest MacMullen, one of very few of Hemingway's friends and hunting companions still alive, was familiar with the Scott. In January 1960, at Papa's request, he sent it to A&F to have the triggers adjusted and the

sling swivels removed. Although he chooses to believe that Papa's death was an accident, MacMullen agrees that the Scott was most likely the gun that caused it.

It is impossible to determine whether Scott or a supplier made the lock provided by the welder. We also don't know what changes may have been made to the sideplates or lockwork over the 44-year production run of the Monte Carlo B. We do know that the remnant screw from the destroyed lock does not exactly fit the hole in the plate from Shelton's

Monte Carlo B (it is slightly larger), but at a time when individual craftsmen tapped and threaded their own screws by hand, this is not unusual. Finally, engraver Charles Lee, formerly of Purdey's, examined these photos as well. He agreed: "It's not a Boss." The remnant looked like a Scott to him also.

Searches of the literature and photographs, as well as interviews, found no evidence that Hemingway had owned a Boss gun. No law enforcement incident reports still exist. Finally came word from Bob Beach: "I have reviewed all [A&F] Boss guns up through 1960 and have not seen any transaction involving Hemingway."

How did the Boss legend begin? Papa had a penchant for nicknames and calling one thing something else, and anyone unfamiliar with fine guns easily could be misled. Perhaps an admirer simply wanted such a famous life to have ended with a famous gun. What is clear is that Papa's Scott gun is nowhere to be found. The pieces that were buried in an Idaho field in 1961 are probably still there. Now, however, they lie beneath the home of Adam West, television's Batman.

*The pieces of the gun that ended Ernest Hemingway's life, after providing him many days of success and pleasure afield.*

Steve Helsley

# VARIOUS:
# ADAMY, DARNE, SARASQUETA, ARRIZABALAGA, 'ALBA'

## AN ADAMY OVER/UNDER

On 16 October 1942 Ernest Hemingway paid Abercrombie & Fitch $275 for a secondhand 12-gauge over/under, Serial No. 29392, made by Gebrüder Adamy; it had been consigned 11 months earlier by a Mrs. W.F. Beal.

In October '42 Ernest was in Cuba organizing *Pilar's* private patrols against German submarines in the Caribbean. Martha Gellhorn, however, then still the third Mrs. Hemingway, arrived in New York City on October 11 after three months of travels around the Caribbean, reporting on the U-boat war for *Collier's* Magazine. She had just been in Washington, DC, briefing Spruille Braden, the US ambassador to Cuba (who was also backing her husband's paramilitary activities), and went to New York for a few days of R&R. Martha then returned to Washington to stay at the White House with her friend Eleanor Roosevelt. By the end of October she was back at home at the Finca Vigía.

Two possibilities come to mind: Ernest flew to New York for a brief conjugal visit—after all, he and Martha had been apart since early July—and, as usual, he dropped in on Abercrombie & Fitch. Or Martha may have bought the gun for him as a homecoming/delayed-birthday present. However, A&F records "Ernest Hemingway" as the buyer, not Mrs. Ernest Hemingway; and she preferred to be known as Martha Gellhorn Hemingway, if not just Martha Gellhorn. And the buyer was staying at the Hotel Lombardy, Ernest's habitual base in Manhattan.

However it happened, the Adamy was probably Hemingway's first German over/under, since he bought the pair of Merkels after the war and the single Merkel, although completed in July 1940, likely didn't get out of Europe until the war ended as well.

For all that the Adamy name is little known, $275 ($3,700 in 2010) for a secondhand gun suggests that it was of some quality. Like Merkel and many other gunmakers, Adamy was in the city of Suhl, on the southern edge of the Thuringian Forest in central Germany. Graced, like Italy's Val Trompia, with thick forests, abundant mountain streams and a rich band of iron ore, by the 14th Century Suhl had also become a center of the metalworking trades. Craftsmen brought their skills from

Liège, in what is now Belgium, and Nürnberg and in 1563 the Duke of Henneberg granted permission for the formation of a gunmaker's guild. Frequent wars and growing civilian demand for firearms fueled the growth of Suhl and its neighbor, Zella-Mehlis. The decades leading up to the First World War were golden years of sporting-gun production in the region, which by 1910 had a gunmaking school (closed in 1942, reopened in 1992) and was home to renowned gunmakers with names

One of Adamy's retail outlets was Sloan's Sporting Goods Company, in New York City. In 1929 Sloan's offered Adamy over/under guns and three-barrel Drillings at prices ranging from $123 to $195. (By comparison, the Browning Superposed listed for $107.50 on its debut in 1931.)

Suhl suffered little damage during the Second World War, and on 3 April 1945 General Patton's Third Army arrived. Civilian arms were confiscated and destroyed—crushed un-

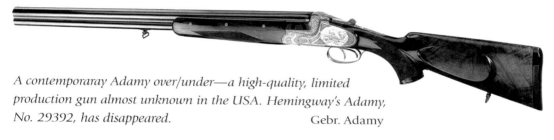

*A contemporaray Adamy over/under—a high-quality, limited production gun almost unknown in the USA. Hemingway's Adamy, No. 29392, has disappeared.*                Gebr. Adamy

such as Jaeger, Meffert, Krieghoff, Walther, Sauer and many others, as well as Adamy and of course Merkel.

The Adamy family arrived in Suhl as French Protestant refugees in about 1790. The first gunsmith was Friedrich Wilhelm Adamy. Two of his sons, Franz, born in 1890, and Albert, eight years younger, went into the trade as well—Franz as an apprentice gunsmith at Greifelt & Co., Albert at Sauer & Sohn. In January 1921 Albert and Franz banded together as Gebrüder Adamy, Gun and Machineworks. Like many of their peers, the brothers cultivated the international market and found customers in Denmark, Italy, Switzerland and the Netherlands as well as Germany.

der Patton's tanks. Gunmakers Krieghoff and Sauer immediately, and presciently, moved into what became West Germany. In July the region was turned over to Russian forces and Suhl found itself in what became the German Democratic Republic—East Germany. For the next 45 years, Adamy and the remaining East German gun companies fell under the supervision of BuHag, the *Büchsenmacher Handelsgesellschaft*, a cooperative that arranged sales and distribution. After the Berlin Wall came down, in 1989, the return to independent operations and free-market capitalism was difficult, but Adamy survived.

As we noted in the previous chapter, Lloyd Arnold wrote this intriguing sentence about one of Ernest's guns: "For some reason or other he reached into his literary character file and called it the 'Adams gun' and said he liked it as well as any he had ever owned." [1] Arnold thought Hemingway was referring to his W. & C. Scott gun, but . . . Adams? Adamy?

Like many other Hemingway guns, the Adamy has vanished. There is no mention of it in Hemingway's own writings and it has not been identified in photos. Adamy's records did not survive World War II, but the firm still builds a few bespoke guns and rifles. Helmut Adamy, who manages the company today, believes that the Beal/Hemingway gun's serial number dates it to his grandfather Albert and grand-uncle Franz and the very early days of Gebr. Adamy.

## PAULINE'S 28-GAUGE DARNE

Midway through *Green Hills of Africa*, on page 95, Hemingway teases us with a throwaway mention of "the small, sharp report of P.O.M.'s 28-gauge."

Poor Old Mama was Pauline Pfeiffer, since 1927 the second Mrs. Hemingway. At the time, she and her husband, not yet known as Papa, were hunting waterfowl in the reedy marshes along the shore of Lake Manyara, in what is now Tanzania, with Charles Thompson and Philip Percival and their gunbearers. Several years later, in the alfalfa fields near Larry and Olive Nordquist's L-Bar-T Ranch in Wyoming, Pauline shot sage hens with a double-barreled 28, presumably the same one, while Ernest used his Model 12 pumpgun.

Patrick Hemingway recalled his mother's

gun well—a French-made Darne side-by-side that Ernest had bought in Paris for shooting with Ben Gallagher: "It had that odd mechanism with the rabbit ears." [2]

Although the basic concepts of modern shotgunning, from one-piece shot cartridges and break-action double guns to shooting gamebirds on the wing (instead of on the ground or in a tree), originated in France, French guns never gained much traction in other markets; from the first, their style simply was too different. At the dawn of the 19th Century, when seminal London gunmaker Joseph Manton was crafting elegantly understated guns with modest touches of checkering and engraving, France's best-known gunmaker, Nicholas-Noel Boutet, was inlaying gold, silver and platinum into every square centimeter of wood and metal on his guns. In decoration as well as in function, the English fine-gun esthetic has since prevailed even in France, but there are still exceptions.

When the break-open breechloader began to gain general acceptance, around 1860, every conceivable way to open, close and lock a gun action was patented. Many of these mechanisms were too impractical, not to say bizarre, to survive, but one oddball from France has now been in production for almost 120 years: the exceptional Darne.

If the conventional side-by-side break-action design, patented in 1833, has any weakness at all, it lies in the hinge pin on which the barrels open and close. With enough use, the hinge can wear, leaving a gap between the barrels and the standing breech. In 1879 a French gunmaker named Regis Darne patented what he thought was a better method: Rather than swing the barrels vertically, he made them pivot laterally to open. But this did not gain favor, and in 1894 he patented what is now known as the Darne action, that "odd mechanism with the rabbit ears." The gun barrels are solidly fixed, and it is the breech-block that moves—sliding horizontally backward on a pair of rails—to open the chambers. The "rabbit ears" are the ends of a T-shaped toggle lever. With two fingers the shooter pulls the

Bruchet, who continues to make Darne-style guns under his family name.

Until recently, the 28 gauge was regarded as a boys' or ladies' gun because the shot load is relatively small and the recoil is mild. It is in fact ideal for the experienced shooter, which Hemingway certainly was, even by 1930. He may have bought it for himself to shoot with Ben Gallagher, as his son recalled, but it is more likely that such a light, easy-handling shotgun was intended for Pauline. What happened to it is not known.

*A French Darne side-by-side similar to the light 28-gauge gun that Ernest bought in Paris and Pauline Hemingway used on the first safari and then in Wyoming. The barrels are fixed; pulling back the "rabbit ears," behind the barrels, opens the action—sliding the breech-block to the rear, exposing the chambers and cocking the hammers. The mechanism is simple, extremely strong and unusually light.* James D. Julia Auctioneers

lever back, which opens the action and withdraws the spent shells. Then fresh cartridges are inserted and the lever is pushed forward, which shoves the rounds into the chambers and cams the gun shut. It is admirably simple and extremely strong and, because less steel is needed, the Darne action is unusually light in weight.

The design proved very popular in France. Various importers have brought Darnes into the United States and Britain, but with little success. Darne shut down in 1980 and the machinery was sold to an employee, Paul Bruchet. The company is now run by Hervé

## THE SPANISH GUNS

Ernest Hemingway could no more have bypassed Spanish-made guns, in light of his love of that unique country and its people, than he could have spent so much time in northern Italy without acquiring a Beretta, or been an early 20th Century American hunter without owning a Winchester, or gone on safari in East Africa without encountering English double rifles.

In the modern era of double-barreled guns and rifles—that is, since about Hemingway's birth—Spanish makers have learned to build highly refined guns in the English style but at substantially lower prices. The prices are a function of their cost of production, but the similarity in the guns stems from a close similarity in the style of shooting, which was no coincidence. Spain has its own long tradition of big-game hunting, but wingshooting there was consciously patterned after the upper-crust British model.

In the decades leading up to the First World War, English society spent its weekends on lavish shooting parties; estates vied to see which could drive the most pheasants, partridges and grouse over the lines of visiting Guns. Daily bags of more than a thousand birds became possible, which sharpened not only guests' shooting skills but also pushed English shotgun design and gunmaking to new levels. At the time, many Spanish grandees had family ties to the UK and were educated in England, and live-pigeon shooting was arriving in Spain from England.

Spanish sportsmen such as the Duke of Santoña and His Highness King Alfonso XIII, who had become aficionados of British wingshooting, saw an opportunity at home with their native gamebird, the red-legged partridge. In the late 1800s at Ventosilla, his family estate south of Madrid (once the private hunting preserve of the cardinals of Toledo), Santoña began to organize English-style driven shoots. More and more of the great Spanish *fincas*, which belong to the landed aristocracy, adopted this rarified form of hunting. Today, the daily bags of partridge on many of these shoots far exceed the norms in the United Kingdom.

Shooting driven gamebirds anywhere demands dynamic guns built for fast, instinctive handling and tailored to their owners' physical dimensions. Spain's Mediterranean climate added another critical element, something unknown in the UK and northern Europe: heat. Spain's best gunmakers build, in effect, English game guns that can absorb the pounding of high-volume shooting without seizing up when the temperature climbs—but still at just a fraction of the price of comparable guns from London.

One gunmaker in particular flourished at the start of Spain's enthusiastic pursuit of wingshooting in the 20th Century: Victor Sarasqueta, who established his firm in Eibar, in the Basque region of northeastern Spain, in 1883. By 1902 King Alfonso XIII had appointed him a Purveyor to the Royal House of Spain. Alfonso, a friend of London gunmaker Athol Purdey, encouraged Sarasqueta to model his sporting guns after Purdey's, and with well-deserved national pride the King often showed off his Purdeys and his Sarasquetas together.

Late in the 1950s, Ernest Hemingway presented his friend and hunting host Bud Purdy with a 12-gauge Sarasqueta, a high-grade, sidelock-action side-by-side, Serial No. 19196. The name "J.M. Urriola" is inscribed on the bottom of the action body, along with "Sarasqueta" and "Eibar"; the barrels are marked "Parsa" and "Madrid." The gun was shipped, in a fitted leather case embossed with the initials B.P., to Purdy from Abercrombie & Fitch.

Bud—Leonard N. Purdy—is the patriarch of Idaho's Picabo Livestock Company, which his grandfather and grand-uncles founded in

*The beautifully engraved and finished 12-gauge Sarasqueta gun, Serial No. 19196, that Ernest Hemingway gave to Bud Purdy in 1958 or '59. Purdy retired it after Papa died, in 1961; he didn't want Hemingway to know that he had trouble adapting to its double triggers, and in fact preferred to hunt with his Ithaca Model 37 pumpgun. The stock was broken at the wrist in an accident and glued together again. The handscrew on the sideplate makes this a detachable-lock gun, very much in the English style of Holland & Holland of London.*

Andy Kent

1883. Purdy took over the operation in 1943, a few years after Hemingway and Martha Gellhorn began to spend the late summer and fall at the nearby Sun Valley Resort. Purdy was already using a small plane to oversee his family's livestock and acreage, and then to spot ducks for Hemingway and the "tribe," of which he became a member in good standing. (The Purdy property includes some miles of Silver Creek, where Hemingway often hunted ducks and sometimes fished for trout.) Bud Purdy turned 92 in 2010; he still works the ranch and still flies. He hunted with the Sarasqueta decades ago, but he never got comfortable with a double-trigger gun. Today it occupies a place of honor in his home, alongside the Mannlicher-Schoenauer rifle that Mary Hemingway left to him in 1986.

At least one other Hemingway friend received a Spanish gun. *Cosmopolitan* sent a young editor named A.E. Hotchner to Havana in 1948 to try to persuade Hemingway to write for the magazine. Instead of avoidance, Hotchner was met with warmth and generosity that ripened into a strong friendship that lasted the rest of Hemingway's life and significantly altered Hotchner's long life. (Hotchner turned 90 in June 2010 and was then in good health.) Papa never wrote for *Cosmopolitan* and Hotchner soon left the magazine, but the two men became business partners. Neither

*A.E. Hotchner's 12-gauge sidelock Arrizabalaga, Serial No. 7349, made to his measure in the late 1950s as a gift from Ernest Hemingway. To date, the last shot fired from the gun was at a cock pheasant, in Idaho in 1958, by Hemingway himself. Hotchner kept the bird and had it mounted.*

William Hoiles/Griffin & Howe

by inclination or background was Hotchner a hunter, but as he did with many friends Papa insisted that "Hotch" give it a serious try.

In the spring of 1954 Hotchner and Hemingway drove from Venice to Madrid, over the Alps and along the Riviera. As they crossed into northeastern Spain, Papa called for a stop in the town of Eibar, the center of Spain's gunmaking trade, to visit the Arrizabalaga workshop to discuss a gun that was being built for him. Hemingway decided on the spot that Hotchner should have a fine gun too, for hunting with him in Idaho. Pedro Arrizabalaga himself consulted with them about it. "We spent a good deal of time in the shop," Hotchner recalled, "first selecting wood for the stock, then going through the elaborate process of measuring my arm, my hand, my height and weight, the fit of my jaw on a sample stock." [3]

In 1956 Hotchner, Mary and Ernest went to the Arrizabalaga dealer in Madrid, where the gun and its leather case had been sent, for a final fitting. Hotchner returned to New York, but Ernest stayed on. The gun was finished before his departure, so he brought it with him to Cuba.

In the fall of 1958 Hotchner was working on a television screenplay of *For Whom the Bell Tolls* and Hemingway invited him to Idaho to discuss the project and, naturally, to go hunting.

On the last day, Hotchner said, "Ernest switched guns with me so that he could get a feel of mine. The stock was short for him, but in the fading light we flushed one last magnificent cock rooster that soared over us. Ernest dropped him with a single shot. I asked if I could have the bird as a remembrance of that day. Ernest knew a 'wonder' taxidermist in Hailey, and I left the pheasant with him. I picked it up when I left Ketchum and it has soared next to my fireplace ever since." [3]

This was, to date, the last shot fired through Hotchner's gun.

Pedro Arrizabalaga began as an engraver with Casa Ugartechea, another gunmaker in Eibar. In 1944, at the age of 39, he and three other employees split off to establish his own firm, Pedro Arrizabalaga SA. At first his guns were sold only by word of mouth in Spain, but by the early 1970s they had achieved international acclaim and were highly sought after. The ownership changed in 1978 and the company is still in business today, producing a small number of high-quality guns—always in the English mode and not inexpensive, but, in true Spanish style, still far less costly than a London gun.

Lloyd Arnold wrote that in November 1960, in preparing for a day of hunting, Papa took out a pair of "matched double guns that he'd brought from Spain." This struck Arnold as odd: "always a utilitarian, Papa did not go around spending his dough on semi-fancy guns, which these were; when first showing them to me, he was actually embarrassed, or apologetic. He never fired a shot from either of them, abhorred their 'spongy' tandem triggers, and greatly admired their fine English trunk-style leather cases." [1]

Were these also from Arrizabalaga, perhaps the order that Hemingway was discussing when he and Hotchner visited Eibar in 1954?

*Idaho, 1958. Hotchner and Hemingway with mallards taken after that November's notable Indian summer weather and the pheasant hunting had passed. A minor mystery: Hotchner's gun here is not the Arrizabalaga that Hemingway had made for him, nor is it identifiable as one of the Hemingway family guns. It may be a Lefever that had belonged to Gene Van Guilder, who died in a hunting accident in 1939, and then passed to Lloyd Arnold. This photo is the frontispiece of Hotchner's acclaimed biography,* Papa Hemingway. A.E. Hotchner

*Indian Creek, on the Middle Fork of the Salmon River, Idaho, 1939. Sun Valley Resort's chief hunting and fishing guide Taylor Williams admires a trophy mountain goat taken by one of his clients, Woody Gardiner. Williams helped many guests, including Mary and Patrick Hemingway, take their first big-game animals, often loaning them one or another of his two well-known Model 70 Winchester rifles. Shown here is probably the .270; the other was in .257 Roberts caliber. Williams, who was 12 years older than Hemingway, died in 1959. His son Bob gave one of the Model 70s to Lloyd Arnold and the other to Hemingway. That rifle in turn passed to the Larkin family upon Mary Hemingway's death, in 1986, and is now in Europe with the brother of Sean Larkin, who has the Merkel Model 401E.*

Tim Gardiner

## THE DUKE OF ALBA GUN

One of the most intriguing of Hemingway's guns is the "Duke of Alba" shotgun, which Lloyd Arnold, Mary and even Jack Hemingway mention in their memoirs. Pulling together the various descriptions and reminiscences, it was Spanish, a "museum piece" and "obviously built for someone of note"—a 12-gauge side-by-side, ornately engraved and stocked in fancy Circassian walnut, with 30-inch Damascus barrels. In 1941 Hemingway wanted to give it to Lloyd Arnold. Arnold protested that it should stay in his family because it came of personal experience; Ernest grudgingly agreed, noting, however, that his sons were not "nearly ready for it yet." [1]

But in 1946 Hemingway loaned the gun to a guest for a dove shoot in Cuba. The guest's bird boy stumbled while carrying the gun and plugged the barrels with mud. When the guest, evidently unaware of the obstruction, fired it, the barrels were destroyed. Back in Idaho a year later, Papa told Arnold he had not sent it to the maker for repair because he was in bad odor in Franco's Spain due to his passionate support for the losing side during the Civil War of 1936-'39.

In September 1947, while Hemingway was driving his latest Buick Roadmaster from Miami to Sun Valley for the fall hunting season, Cuban soldiers

*Questions will always remain. This photo, from an April 1988* Architectural Digest *article about the Hemingway house in Idaho, shows what appears to be Hemingway's Winchester Model 77 .22 rifle and Mary's two 20-gauge Model 21 shotguns. Also included, however, is a semi-automatic shotgun and what looks to be a third Model 21—by the diameter of their barrels, both appear to be 12-gauges. We have found no record of or reference to these guns.*

raided the Finca Vigía, looking for illicit guns and ammunition that could fall into the hands of revolutionaries. Mary was packing to fly to Idaho with half a dozen of their guns, which they had decided was safer than transporting them across the country in a car. She tried to deflect the searchers, but the house was all but overflowing with weaponry:

"A small truck had backed up the driveway and with surprising efficiency the little army unit filled it with rifles and shotguns, the Duke of Alba's shotgun which E. had somehow acquired during the Spanish Civil War and Ernest's favorite old Winchester pump gun among them, U.S. and German army pistols and hundreds, if not thousands, of shells and unopened boxes of rifle ammunition in various dimensions, our wicker wastebaskets of shotgun shells looking incongruous and cozy among the guns.

"'You must come with us now,' the lieutenant said. . . ." [4]

Mary was able to prove that everything was legitimate and to depart for Idaho. The Duke of Alba gun must have been returned, for eldest son Jack Hemingway used it several times when he visited his father and stepmother in Cuba—once on a Martini-fueled father-and-son buzzard shoot on the roof of the tower that Mary had added to the Finca. Since this took place in the mid-1950s, Hemingway finally had had the gun's barrels replaced.

Jack believed that Papa had "liberated" the gun from one of the Duke's residences as spoils of war. The Dukedom of Alba is one of the oldest and wealthiest in Europe; the family gunrooms would have held nothing but the best. Jacobo Fitz-James Stuart, the 17th Duke of Alba, was General Francisco Franco's ambassador to England. During Spain's civil war, which amounted to a practice run for World War II, Russian-led Communist forces fighting on the Republican side seized the Duke's palace of Liria, which the German Condor Legion then bombed. It is possible that the gun could have been looted from the palace; it is also possible that Hemingway gilded the lily and gave the mysterious gun some extra provenance.

Ernest Hemingway was a restless globe-trotter who used, bought, borrowed, loaned out, gave away and probably traded guns throughout his life. Questions about them will always remain. In 1930 he wrote to a friend that he was a novice when it came to rifles, but he owned 10 shotguns. If this was true, we have only been able to identify three from that time period. What were the other seven? Was one of them his very first shotgun: the single-shot 20-gauge that his grandfather presented him on his 10th birthday, more than a century ago? What became of it? A cheap utility gun, it may have finally

rusted away in a barn somewhere.

Like many veterans, Hemingway probably had souvenir guns from both World Wars—the military Mannlicher that Leicester wrote of, or captured Wehrmacht pistols, the Colt .45 semi-autos that Americans carried, perhaps a German Drilling or a French shotgun or two. Exactly what weapons was he issued in 1942 for cruising against German raiders in the Caribbean? Was his Thompson mixed in with them, and then jettisoned over the side in '58?

Did he really own a pair of light, 25-inch Purdey shotguns, as he claimed in one of his letters to Milford Baker and Hotchner seemed to corroborate? No trace of them has been found. Hotchner also wrote, in *True*, September 1971, that Hemingway had a Winchester Model 70 African-model bolt-action rifle in .458 Magnum; again, no other record or evidence. Did Papa have a "heavy Colt target pistol" and a Colt Officer's Model .22 revolver with a six-inch barrel, as friends recalled?

What became of the Sweet 16 Browning autoloader that Hemingway all but confiscated from Slim Hawks in 1946, and Professor Seward's memorial Woodsman pistol, proudly displayed in his den? Who unsuspectingly bought Woodsman No. 12072 in Nairobi, late in the '90s? Is it rattling around in the glove box of a dusty Land Cruiser somewhere in Kenya? What happened to the second set of barrels for Martha's Model 21? Where did the notion of the Boss suicide gun originate? Did you acquire a worn Model 12 with an odd bird's-eye-maple stock in New York's

*Farewell. On the deck of the "Silver Creek Rod & Gun Club," Picabo, Idaho, late 1959. From left: Gary Cooper, Bud Purdy, Papa, Barbara Powell, John Powell, Ruth Purdy. Cooper holds what appears to be Papa's Beretta S3 over/under, with its Kersten fasteners and distinctive forend. Bud cradles his favorite shotgun, an Ithaca Model 37 12-gauge pump. Hemingway, eyeglasses off for the camera, has his Scott pigeon gun, Ruth a Winchester Model 62 .22 rifle. On the table lies another .22 rifle, probably the semi-automatic Model 77 Winchester.* Purdy Family Collection

western Catskills around 1980? Is its serial number 525488?

If you have information about these guns, please contact the publisher of this book.

When we were crying in our beer about these and more unanswered—and probably unanswerable—questions with a veteran Hemingway scholar, she smiled and said, "See? There's never an end to questions and doubts, as one tries to get the facts straight. Everyone who ever had anything to do with Ernest Hemingway had a different story to tell about everything. Even he told different stories about everything."

# CITATIONS

## INTRODUCTION

1. Hotchner, A.E. (1971). "The Guns of Hemingway." *True*, September 1971.

## THE MODEL 12 PUMPGUNS

1. Hemingway, Ernest. (2005). *Under Kilimanjaro*. Kent, OH: Kent State University Press. p. 326
2. Baker, Carlos. (1981). *Ernest Hemingway: Selected Letters 1917 - 1961*. New York, NY: Charles Scribner's Sons. p. 325
3. Hemingway, Patrick. (2009)
4. Hemingway, Ernest. (1934). "Notes on Dangerous Game: The Third Tanganyika Letter." *Esquire*, July 1934
5. Arnold, Lloyd R. (1968). *High on the Wild with Hemingway* (1st ed.). Caldwell, ID: The Caxton Printers. pp. 32, 395

## THE BROWNING SUPERPOSED

1. Browning Arms Co. Catalog, 1931
2. Arnold, Lloyd R. (1968). *High on the Wild with Hemingway* (1st ed.). Caldwell, ID: The Caxton Printers. pp. 32, 218

## TWO BROWNING AUTOMATIC 5s

1. Ugarov, Andrey. (2010)
2. Baker, Carlos. (1981). *Ernest Hemingway: Selected Letters 1917 - 1961*. New York, NY: Charles Scribner's Sons. p. 345

## THE WINCHESTER MODEL 21 SHOTGUNS

1. Arnold, Lloyd R. (1968). *High on the Wild with Hemingway* (1st ed.). Caldwell, ID: The Caxton Printers. p. 94
2. Hemingway, Mary. (1976). *How It Was*. New York, NY: Alfred Knopf. p. 184

## THE BERETTA S3 OVER/UNDER

1. Hemingway, Mary. (1976). *How It Was*. New York, NY: Alfred Knopf. p. 258
2. Hemingway, Ernest. (2005). *Under Kilimanjaro*. Kent, OH: Kent State University Press. p. 392

## THE GRIFFIN & HOWE .30-06 SPRINGFIELD

1. Baker, Carlos. (1981). *Ernest Hemingway: Selected Letters 1917 - 1961*. New York, NY: Charles Scribner's Sons. p. 324
2. Hemingway, Mary. (1976). *How It Was*. New York, NY: Alfred Knopf. pp. 408, 420
3. Hemingway, Ernest. (2005). *Under Kilimanjaro*. Kent, OH: Kent State University Press. p. 257

## MANNLICHER-SCHOENAUER RIFLES

1. Hemingway, Leicester. (1961). *My Brother, Ernest Hemingway*. Cleveland, OH: The World Publishing Company. pp. 57, 14

2. Hemingway, Ernest. (1934). "Notes on Dangerous Game: The Third Tanganyika Letter". *Esquire*, July 1934

3. Arnold, Lloyd R. (1968). *High on the Wild with Hemingway* (1st ed.). Caldwell, ID: The Caxton Printers. pp. 32, 120

4. Hemingway, Mary. (1976). *How It Was.* New York, NY: Alfred Knopf. pp. 413, 466, 593

5. Hemingway, Ernest. (2005). *Under Kilimanjaro.* Kent, OH: Kent State University Press. pp. 40, 211

## THE .577 NITRO EXPRESS & OTHER DOUBLE RIFLES

1. Hemingway, Ernest. (2005). *Under Kilimanjaro.* Kent, OH: Kent State University Press. pp. 321, 216

2. Aschan, Ulf. (1987). *The Man Whom Women Loved — The Life of Bror Blixen.* New York, NY: St. Martin's Press. p. 135

3. Hemingway, Ernest. (1934). "Notes on Dangerous Game: The Third Tanganyika Letter." *Esquire*, July 1934.

4. Hemingway, Leicester. (1961). *My Brother, Ernest Hemingway.* Cleveland, OH: The World Publishing Company. pp. 137, 154

5. Zaphiro, Denis and Bingham, Worth. (1963). "Hemingway's Last Safari". *Rogue*, February 1963.

6. Hemingway, Ernest. (1987). *Green Hills of Africa.* New York, NY: Collier/Macmillan. pp. 42, 86

7. Hemingway, Mary. (1976). *How It Was.* New York, NY: Alfred Knopf. p. 291

8. Hemingway, Patrick. (2009).

## THREE (FOUR?) COLT WOODSMAN PISTOLS

1. Hemingway, Ernest. (2005). *Under Kilimanjaro.* Kent, OH: Kent State University Press. p. 50

2. Hemingway, Ernest. (1938). "My Pal the Gorilla Gargantua." *Ken*, 28 July 1938.

3. Seward, William. (1969). *My Friend Ernest Hemingway.* Cranbury, NJ: A.S. Barnes and Co.

4. Baker, Carlos. (1981). *Ernest Hemingway: Selected Letters 1917 - 1961.* New York, NY: Charles Scribner's Sons. p. 659

## THE MODEL 61 WINCHESTER & OTHER .22 RIFLES

2. Baker, Carlos. (1981). *Ernest Hemingway: Selected Letters 1917 - 1961.* New York, NY: Charles Scribner's Sons. p. 26

3. Hemingway, Ernest and Baker, Milford J. correspondence. (1930). Princeton University Library.

4. Hemingway, Mary. (1976). *How It Was.* New York, NY: Alfred Knopf. p. 262

5. Hemingway, Leicester. (1961). *My Brother, Ernest Hemingway.* Cleveland, OH: The World Publishing Company. p. 75

6. Hemingway, Valerie. (2004). *Running with the Bulls - My Years with the Hemingways.* New York, NY: Ballantine Books. p. 40

7. Hotchner, A.E. (1971). "The Guns of Hemingway." *True*, September 1971

## A THOMPSON SUBMACHINE GUN

1. Smith, Anthony. (2003). *Machine Gun.* New York, NY: St. Martin's Press.

## A BIG-BORE MAUSER, OR TWO

1.  Hemingway, Ernest and Baker, Milford J. correspondence. (1930). Princeton University Library
2.  Taylor, John. (1994). *African Rifles and Cartridges*. Long Beach, CA: Safari Press.
3.  Baker, Carlos. (1981). *Ernest Hemingway: Selected Letters 1917 - 1961*. New York, NY: Charles Scribner's Sons.

## THE W. & C. SCOTT & SON PIGEON GUN

1.  Baker, Carlos. (1981). *Ernest Hemingway: Selected Letters 1917 - 1961*. New York, NY: Charles Scribner's Sons. p. 345
2.  Hemingway, Jack. (1986). *Misadventures of a Fly Fisherman - My Life With and Without Papa*. Dallas, TX: Taylor Publishing Co. p. 87
3.  Hemingway, Mary. (1976). *How It Was*. New York, NY: Alfred Knopf. p. 213
4.  Arnold, Lloyd R. (1968). *High on the Wild with Hemingway* (1st ed.). Caldwell, ID: The Caxton Printers. p. 219

## VARIOUS

1.  Arnold, Lloyd R. (1968). *High on the Wild with Hemingway* (1st ed.). Caldwell, ID: The Caxton Printers. pp. 218, 309, 141
2.  Hemingway, Patrick. (2009).
3.  Hotchner, A.E. (2010).
4.  Hemingway, Mary. (1976). *How It Was*. New York, NY: Alfred Knopf. p. 239

# BIBLIOGRAPHY

Adler, Dennis. (2006). *Winchester Shotguns*. Edison, NJ: Chartwell Books, Inc.

Anderson, Donald. (2008). Personal communications.

Arnold, Lloyd R. (1968). *High on the Wild with Hemingway* (1st ed.). Caldwell, ID: The Caxton Printers.

Aschan, Ulf. (1987). *The Man Whom Women Loved — The Life of Bror Blixen*. New York, NY: St. Martin's Press.

Baker, Carlos. (1967). *By-Line: Ernest Hemingway: Selected Articles and Dispatches of Four Decades*. New York, NY: Scribner's.

Baker, Carlos. (1981). *Ernest Hemingway: Selected Letters 1917 - 1961*. New York, NY: Charles Scribner's Sons.

Baker, Max. (1899). "Rifles in India." *Arms & Explosives*, September 1899, 135. .

Baker, Max. (1916). "The Late Mr. John Rigby." *Arms & Explosives*, December 1916.

Brophy, William S. (1989). *Marlin Firearms*. Mechanicsburg, PA: Stackpole.

Brown, Nigel. (2005). *British Gunmakers* (Vol. Two - Birmingham, Scotland and the Regions). London: Quiller Press.

Browning Arms Co. (1931). *Browning Arms Co. Catalog*. St. Louis, MO.

Bull, Bartle. (1988). *Safari: A Chronicle of Adventure*. New York, NY: Carroll & Graf.

Butterfields Auctioneers. (1997). *Sporting Guns Sale Catalog*, 17 November 1997. San Francisco, CA.

Calabi, Silvio. (2007). "The.470 Nitro Express." *Sports Afield*, June-July 2007, 69-73.

Capstick, Peter Hathaway. (1984). *Safari, The Last Adventure*. New York, NY: Macmillan.

Crawford, J.A. and Whately, P.G. (1985). *The History of W. & C. Scott Gunmakers* (2nd ed.). London: Rowland Ward.

Crudgington, I.M. and Baker, David. (1989). *The British Shotgun* (Vol. II — 1871-1890). Shedfield Hampshire, UK: Ashford.

Curtis, Charles C. (2002). *Systeme Lefaucheux*. Santa Ana, CA: Armslore Press.

Dallas, Donald. (2003). *Holland & Holland, The Royal Gunmakers.* London: Quiller Press.

Eastman, Matt. (1999). *Browning Sporting Arms of Distinction.* Huntington Beach, CA: Safari Press.

Ellis, John. (1987). *The Social History of the Machine Gun* (3rd ed.). London: The Cresset Library.

Ezell, Edward. (1993). *Small Arms of the World.* New York, NY: Barnes & Noble Books.

Fussell, Paul. (1975). *The Great War and Modern Memory.* New York, NY: Oxford University Press.

Griffin & Howe. (1928). *Rifle Makers and Sportsmen's Equipment Catalog, 1928.* New York, NY.

Haven, Charles T. & Belden, Frank A. (1940). *A History of the Colt Revolver.* New York, NY: Bonanza Books.

Hemingway, Ernest. (1934). "Notes on Dangerous Game: The Third Tanganyika Letter." *Esquire,* July 1934.

Hemingway, Ernest. (1938). "My Pal the Gorilla Gargantua." *Ken,* 28 July 1938.

Hemingway, Ernest. (1938). "The Short Happy Life of Francis Macomber." In *The Short Stories of Ernest Hemingway.* New York, NY: Scribner's.

Hemingway, Ernest. (1954). "Safari." *Look,* 26 January 1954.

Hemingway, Ernest. (1954). "The Christmas Gift" Part I. *Look,* 20 April 1954.

Hemingway, Ernest. (1954). "The Christmas Gift" Part II. *Look,* 4 May 1954.

Hemingway, Ernest. (1967). *By-Line: Ernest Hemingway: Selected Articles and Dispatches of Four Decades.* (William White, ed.) New York, NY: Scribner's.

Hemingway, Ernest. (1987). *Green Hills of Africa.* New York, NY: Collier/Macmillan.

Hemingway, Ernest. (1987). *The Garden of Eden.* New York, NY: Collier Books.

Hemingway, Ernest. (1999). *True at First Light.* (Patrick Hemingway, ed.) New York, NY: Scribner.

Hemingway, Ernest. (2005). *Under Kilimanjaro.* Kent, OH: Kent State Univ. Press.

Hemingway, E. & Baker, M. J. (1930). Ernest Hemingway and Milford J. Baker correspondence. Princeton University Library.

Hemingway, Ernest. (2001). (Sean Hemingway, ed.) *Hemingway on Hunting.* Guilford, CT: Globe Pequot Press.

Hemingway, H. & Brennen, C. (2003). *Hemingway in Cuba.* New York, NY: Rugged Land.

Hemingway, Jack. (1986). *Misadventures of a Fly Fisherman - My Life With and Without Papa.* Dallas, TX: Taylor Publishing Co.

Hemingway, Leicester. (1961). *My Brother, Ernest Hemingway.* Cleveland, OH: The World Publishing Company.

Hemingway, Mary. (1976). *How It Was.* New York, NY: Alfred Knopf.

Hemingway, Patrick (2009). Personal communication.

Hemingway, Valerie. (2004). *Running with the Bulls - My Years with the Hemingways.* New York, NY: Ballantine Books.

Herne, Brian. (1999). *White Hunters.* New York, NY: Henry Holt & Co.

Hotchner, A. E. (1971). "The Guns of Hemingway." *True,* September 1971.

Hotchner, A. E. (2010). Personal communication.

Hoyem, George A. (1985). *The History and Development of Small Arms Ammunition* (III). Tacoma, WA: Armory Publications.

John P. Moore's Sons. (1886). Job Sheet. New York, NY.

Kerasote, Ted. (1999). "The Untouchable Wild." *Audubon,* September-October 1999.

Larkin, Sean. (2010) Personal communications.

Livingston, Roxanne Theisen. (2009). Personal communications.

Lyons, Leonard. (1953). "A Day in Town with Hemingway." *New York Post,* 26 June 1953.

Madis, George. (1961). *The Winchester Book.* Dallas, TX: George Madis.

Madis, George. (1984). *Winchester Dates of Manufacture 1849-1984.* Brownsboro, TX: Art & Reference House.

Masters, Don A. (2002). *The House of Churchill.* Long Beach, CA: Safari Press.

McIntosh, Michael. (1989). *Best Guns.* Camden, ME: Countrysport Press.

Murcot, Ray M. (2007). *U.S. Sharpshooters: Berdan's Civil War Elite.* Mechanicsburg, PA: Stackpole Books.

Ondaatje, Christopher. (2004). *Hemingway in Africa.* New York, NY: The Overlook Press.

Parker, Ian. (2009-'10). Personal communication.

Petzal, David. (1985). "Model 12—The Perfect Repeater." *Sporting Classics,* May/June 1985.

Purdy, Leonard N. ("Bud"). 2009-'10. Personal communication.

Reynolds, Michael. (1986). *The Young Hemingway*. Oxford, UK: Basil Blackwell Ltd.

Reynolds, Michael. (1997). *Hemingway: The 1930s*. New York, NY: W.W. Norton.

Reynolds, Michael. (2000). *Hemingway: The Final Years*. New York, NY: W.W. Norton.

Roberts, MacNeil. (1958). "Hemingway Talks About Guns." *Gunsport*, April 1958.

Roosevelt, Theodore. (1910). *African Game Trails*. New York, NY: Scribner's.

Schefelbein, Ted. "Le Bon Vieux Darne." *The Double Gun Journal*, Summer 1996.

Schwing, Ned. (1996). *Browning Superposed, John M. Browning's Last Legacy*. Iola, WI: Krause Publishing.

Schwing, Ned. (2000). *2001 Standard Catalog of Firearms*. Iola, WI: Krause Publications.

Schwing, Ned. (2005). *Winchester's Finest, the Model 21*. Iola, WI: Krause Publications.

Seward, William. (1969). *My Friend Ernest Hemingway*. Cranbury, NJ: A.S. Barnes and Co.

Smith, Anthony. (2003). *Machine Gun*. New York, NY: St. Martin's Press.

Sommer, François. (1953). *Man and Beast in Africa* (Edward Fitzgerald, Trans.). London: Herbert Jenkins.

Speed, Jon, Schmid, W. and Herrmann, R. (1997). *Original Oberndorf Sporting Rifles*. Ontario, Canada: Collector Grade Publications.

Steinhart, Edward I. (2006). *Black Poachers/White Hunters*. Athens, OH: Ohio Univ. Press.

Stoeger Arms Corp. (1940). *Arms, Ammunition & Shooting Accessories Catalog*. New York, NY.

Stoeger Arms Corp. (1929). *Stoeger Arms & Ammunition Catalog* No. 26. New York, NY.

Stoeger Arms Corp. (1940). *Shooter's Bible*. New York, NY.

Tate, Douglas. (1997). *Birmingham Gunmakers*. Long Beach, CA: Safari Press, Inc.

Taylor, John. (reprinted 1994). *African Rifles and Cartridges*. Long Beach, CA: Safari Press.

Teasdale-Buckell, G.T. (1900). *Experts on Guns and Shooting*. London: Sampson, Low, Marston & Co., Inc.

Theisen, Earl (1999). "The Last Safari." *Audubon*, September-October 1999.

Tregear, Anthony (2009). Personal communication.

Ugarov, Andrey. (2010). Personal communication.

unknown. (1961). "The Hero of the Code." *Time*, 14 July 1961.

unknown (1881). Obituary - William W. Winchester. *New York Times*.

Walter, John. (1979). *The German Rifle*. London: Arms and Armour Press.

Watrous, George R. (1966). *The History of Winchester Firearms 1866 - 1966* (3rd ed.). New Haven, CT: Winchester-Western Press.

Whelen, Townsend (1934). "United States Rifle, Caliber.30." *American Rifleman*, August 1934.

Williamson, Harold. (1963). *Winchester, The Gun That Won the West*. New York, NY: A.S. Barnes & Co., Inc.

Wilson, R.L. (1991). *Winchester, An American Legend*. Edison, NJ: Chartwell Books, Inc.

Wilson, R.L. (2000). *The World of Beretta*. New York, NY: Random House.

Winchester Repeating Arms Co. (1911). Catalog 77. New Haven, CT.

Winchester-Western. (1965). *Winchester Model 21 Catalog*. New Haven, CT.

Zaphiro, Denis and Bingham, Worth (1963). "Hemingway's Last Safari." *Rogue*, February 1963.

# INDEX

.30-30 Winchester 122

.300 H&H Magnum 10

.375 H&H Magnum 78, 79

.404 Jeffery 138, 139

.404 Rimless Nitro Express 138

.416 Rigby 78, 135

.45 ACP 133

.450 BPE 102

.450 Nitro Express 103, 104

.450 No. 2 78, 88, 104

.470 Nitro Express 78, 97, 102, 104, 105

.505 Gibbs 86, 134, 135, 136, 137

.577 Nitro Express 93–99, 106, 107

"Snows of Kilimanjaro" 6

"The Short Happy Life of Francis Macomber" 89

"The Shot" 40

20th Hussars 106

*A Farewell to Arms* 20, 153

Abercrombie & Fitch 8, 16, 22, 46, 47, 50, 51, 58, 60, 61, 66, 67, 74–76, 81, 91–93, 113, 114, 119, 126, 129, 136, 150, 154, 158

Aberdare Mountains 113

*Across the River and Into the Trees* 150

Adams gun 150, 156

Afghanistan 103

Alba, Duke of 162, 163

Angelini & Bernardon 150

Anson & Deeley 64, 96, 100, 146

Anson, William 96

Apel, Dietrich 3

Armeria Caccia 60

Arnold, Lloyd 3, 9, 20, 21, 23, 25–27, 29, 32, 40, 41, 47, 70, 77, 79, 83, 86, 90, 92, 119, 121, 140, 144, 150, 155, 160–162

Arnold, Tillie 90

Arrizabalaga 154, 155, 157, 159–161, 163, 165

Auto-Ordnance Corporation 131

Babati 98

Baker, Milford 8, 75, 78, 84, 102, 112, 122, 135, 164

Barnett, Lawrence 121

Baruch, Bernard 61

Battersea 141

Battle of the Marne 106

Bayard 66

Beach, Bob 3, 8, 150, 153

Beal, Mrs. W.F. 154

Beavertail forend 44, 46, 47

Beretta, Pietro 62

Bimini 130

Birdshot 10, 13

Birmingham 42, 63, 95, 106, 146

Blixen, Bror 93, 98, 101

Blue heron 123

Bluefin tuna 130

*Bockflinte* 55

Boer War 106

Boettiger, John 45

Bogardus, Capt. Adam Henry 142, 145

Bombay Castle 103

Bonham's 83, 90

Booth, Chester 129

Boss & Company 24

Boutet, Nicholas-Noel 156

Boxed pigeons 54, 140, 141

Boxlock action 28, 44, 64, 66

Braden, Spruille 106, 154

Brescia 61, 62

Brokaw, William Gould 51, 56

Browning, John M. 24, 26, 27, 34, 35, 41–43, 63, 66, 133

Browning, Val Allen 28, 30

Bruchet, Paul 157

Buckshot 10, 13, 18

Buffalo Bill Historic Center 49

BuHag 155

Bullfighting 31, 40, 125

Burma 136

Burton, Frank F. 43

Butterfield & Butterfield 90

Cape buffalo 72, 73, 95, 99, 100, 135

Capone, Al 132

Capstick, Peter Hathaway 126

Carver, William F. "Doc" 142

Cast off 58

Cast on 58

Castro, Fidel 31

Cat Cay 130

Chassepot 82

Chicago 5, 132, 148

Christy, Stephen H. 93, 106, 107

Church Stretton 93, 106

Churchill, E.J. 53

Churchill, Robert 54

Civil War, American 42, 146

Civil War, Spanish 163

Clay pigeon 34, 142

Club des Cazadores 15, 17, 31, 47, 51, 58, 65, 67, 101, 140, 144

Codroipo 5, 60, 140, 150

Cody Firearms Museum 46, 49

*Collier's* 37, 125, 136, 154

Colt, Samuel 118, 135

Condor Legion 164

Connecticut Shotgun Manufacturing Co. 46

Converse, William W. 42

Cook, Charles 130

Cooper, Dick 98

Cooper, Gary 27, 165

Cooper, Veronica 12

Cordite 94, 104

Corncob forend 13, 16

*Cosmopolitan* 136, 159

Crossbolt 44, 55, 140, 148

Crystal cocking indicators 148

Curry Mansion Inn 93, 107, 108

Cutts Compensator 36, 37, 133

Danby-Smith, Valerie 3, 125

Darne, Regis 157

*Death in the Afternoon* 125

Debba 114

Dechevrieux, Michael 3, 150

Deeley, John 96

Demibloc 64

Distinguished Service Order 106

Dominguin, Luis Miguel 126

Dos Passos, John 30, 130

Dreyse 82

*Drilling* 55, 155, 164

Droplock 94, 96

Dunabeitia, Juan 120

EAPHA 18, 71

Edward VII 96

Eibar 158, 160

Eisenhower, Dwight D. 56

Elephant 6, 88, 94, 99–101, 103, 108, 126, 135, 138

Elliott, Rodney 109

*Esquire* 4, 6, 7, 32, 90, 124, 133

Etchen, Rudy 20

Fabrique Nationale d'Armes de Guerre 26

Fairview Lodge 52

Federal Migratory Bird Act 27

Finca Vigía 5, 57, 65, 73, 86, 90, 101, 120, 126, 142, 154, 163

Fitzgerald, F. Scott 30, 52

Flex-Choke 20, 21

FN 26, 28

*For Whom the Bell Tolls* 27, 38, 41, 119, 160

Forli 62

Fox 42, 55

Franchetti, Baron Nanyuki 60, 141

Franchetti, Bianca 106

Franco, Gen. Francisco 164

Franco-Prussian War 82

Fuentes, Gregorio 108

G.C. 80, 81, 87, 97, 99, 111

Gagarin, Yuri 56

Gallagher, Ben 30, 32, 140, 144, 156, 157

Garand rifle 71, 73

*Garden of Eden, The* 6

Gardiners Island 37, 77, 101

Gardone 62

Gibbs, George 135

Gingrich, Arnold 32, 82

Gooding, Tom 29, 40

Gould, Jay 51, 59

Gras 82

*Great Gatsby, The* 52

Greeley, Dr. Margaret 3, 117, 120

Greeley, Horace IV 117, 120

*Green Hills of Africa* 3, 6, 16, 69, 70, 78, 90, 108, 112, 121, 156

Greener 55, 66, 140, 145, 148

Griffin & Howe 78, 79, 81, 84–85, 89, 90, 108, 112, 121, 122, 136

Griffin, Seymour 74, 76

Grizzly bear 75, 78, 118

Guest, Winston 31, 101, 106, 108

Gun Club, The 141

*Guns* 117, 120

*Gunsport* 7

Hague Convention of 1899 71

Hale, William 66, 67

Harriman, Averell 39

Hartford 63, 127

Havana 5, 49, 65, 73, 90, 91, 106, 120, 144, 159

Hawks, "Slim" 36, 37, 40, 124, 164

Hawks, Howard 12, 36, 40

Hemingway, Anson 6

Hemingway, Clarence 41

Hemingway, Gregory "Gigi" 4, 9, 15, 31, 48, 49, 125, 127, 144

Hemingway, Hadley Richardson 30, 123

Hemingway, Jack (John) 9, 25, 31, 144, 162–164

Hemingway, Leicester 72, 84, 89, 102, 112, 123, 164

Hemingway, Martha Gellhorn 23, 31, 38, 39, 41, 47, 90, 91, 101, 154, 159

Hemingway, Mary Welsh 39, 48, 51, 91

Hemingway, Patrick 3, 4, 9, 16, 17, 31, 47, 49,

51, 57, 75, 77, 81, 92, 95, 108, 111, 127, 129, 131, 156, 162

Hemingway, Pauline Pfeiffer 20, 31, 39, 75, 80, 85, 86, 89–92, 102, 108, 121, 138, 139, 156, 157

Hemingway, Sean 4

Henry rifle 42

Henry VIII 62

High Wall Winchester 24

Hinge pin 28, 43, 54, 64, 156

HMS *Kenya* 113

Hoff, Einar 3, 54

Hoffmann Arms 138

Holland & Holland 51, 54, 66, 78, 95, 98, 148, 159

Hollow-point 112, 118

Home, Roy 111

Hong Kong 136

Hoover, J. Edgar 132

Hotchner, A.E. 3, 5, 8, 121, 125, 126, 128, 159–161, 164

*How It Was* 38

Industrial Revolution 62

Irish Republican Army 81

J. Rigby & Co. 103, 134

Jaeger 155

Jeffery, William J. 138

Jenkins, Howell 121

John F. Kennedy Library 4, 6, 7, 9, 12, 15, 17, 19, 21, 25–27, 29, 31, 36, 42, 45, 47, 48, 57, 71–73, 75, 77, 79, 81, 85–89, 95, 97, 99, 101, 110, 115, 116, 119, 124, 127, 133, 141–143, 145, 147, 149

Johnson, Thomas Crosley 33

Julia, James D. 23, 33, 47, 49, 51, 69, 117, 123, 126, 129, 131, 135, 157

Kaiser Wilhelm I 82

Kajiado District 18, 87, 114

Kalashnikov, Mikhail 135

*Kansas City Star, The* 51

Kechler 5, 60, 140, 141, 150

*Ken* 4, 7

Kenya Bunduki 102, 109, 111

Kenya Regiment 112

Kersten 55, 57, 64, 65, 165

Ketchum 39, 40, 81, 91, 119, 150, 160

Key West 7, 13, 20, 31, 38, 68, 70, 77, 93, 107, 108, 130, 134, 138

Khrushchev, Nikita 56

Kikuyu 112–114

King Alfonso XIII 158

King's African Rifles 112

Krag-Jørgensen 83

Krieghoff 3, 155

Kusmit, Nick 49

Lake Manyara 156

Lake Walloon 123

Lang, Joseph 61, 104

Lanham, Gen. Charles T. 33, 37, 125

Larkin, Charles 40, 50, 59

Larkin, Gioia 50, 59

Larkin, Sean 3, 59, 129, 162

L-Bar-T Ranch 77, 156

Lee, Charles 3, 153

Lee, James Paris 83

Leeds, William Bateman 130, 131

Lefever 42, 161

Length of pull 38, 46, 47

Leopard 13, 17, 18, 20, 72, 81, 92, 100, 114, 116

Lever-action 7, 11, 33, 41, 42, 43, 121–123, 127, 128

Lewis, George 43

Liège 63, 155

*Life* 7, 120, 150

Lion 17, 51, 70, 78, 80, 88, 94, 97, 100, 104,
     105, 114, 116, 136

Liria 164

Long Island 22, 52, 101

*Look* 6, 7, 81, 93, 99, 115, 116, 120, 124

Louis, Joe 118, 122

Lowe, William 114, 115, 120

Lyman sight 76, 135

Lyons, Leonard 93

Machakos 114

Mackay, Clarence 53

MacLeish, Archibald 138

MacMullen, Forrest "Duke" 3, 40, 150

Magnum Mauser 135

Maharajah of Cooch Behar 126

Málaga 125, 126

*Man at Arms* 117, 120

Mannlicher, Ferdinand 41, 84

Manton, Joseph 156

Mao Tse Tung 56

Mapes Auction Gallery 60, 66

Marcheno 62

Marchica, Joe 120

Markham, Beryl 93, 101

Marlin 130, 133

Marlin (Firearms Co.) 121–123, 128

Marne River 112

Martini-Henry 103

Marvel Mystery Oil 17

Masai 114, 124

Masters, Don 53, 54

Matterelli, Ennio 66

Mau Mau 112–114

Mauser 16, 26, 71, 74, 77, 82–84, 86, 134–139

Maxim, Hiram 26, 131

Mayfair 96

Meffert 155

Mella River 61

Middle Ages 61

Milan 61, 63

*Moana* 130

Model 1897 14, 33, 42, 121, 123, 128

Model 1911 27, 62, 118, 133

Mombasa 66, 102, 120

Monobloc 61, 64, 66

Montana 6, 13, 38, 70, 81, 128

Monte Carlo B 140, 148, 151–153

Moore & Harris 146

Moore, John P. 43

Mueller, Cy 61

Murphy, Sara 130

Nairobi 3, 7, 102, 108, 109, 112–115, 120,
     139, 164, 178

Nasser, Gamal Abdel 56

National Board for the Promotion of Rifle
     Practice 74, 131, 133

National Firearms Act 11

National Rifle Association 69, 74, 76

Needle-fire 82

New Haven 13, 41, 42, 47, 122

*New York Post, The* 93

*New Yorker, The* 7

Newman, Warren 3, 46

Nick Adams 6

Nitro Express 55, 64, 78, 86, 93–97, 99
     101–105, 107, 118, 122, 133, 137, 138, 146

Nodop, John 3, 22

Nordquist 38, 75, 82, 156

Norris, Samuel 82

Nürnberg 155

Oakley, Annie 123

Oberndorf 82, 135, 136, 172, 178

Old Dominion University 120

Old Hats Tavern 141

Old Hornsey Wood House 141

Olin, John M. 45, 46

Olympics 66, 142

Open sights 92, 98

Ordoñez, Antonio 125, 126

P. Webley & Son 113, 148

Pakistan 103

Paris Exposition of 1900 84

Parker Bros. 42

Parker, Ian 3, 109, 111, 112

Patterson, John Henry 136

Peirce, Waldo 13, 30

Perazzi, Daniele 66

Percival, Blayney 136

Percival, Philip 16, 18, 70, 71, 78, 88, 92, 102, 104, 109, 111, 136, 139, 156

Perfect Repeater 14, 33

Petitclerc, Denne Bart 49

Pfeiffer, "Uncle Gus" 18, 20, 34, 138

Pieper, Henri 64, 66

Pigeon gun 101, 140, 141, 143, 144, 145, 147, 149, 151, 155, 165

Piggott, Arkansas 20, 31, 32

*Pilar* 37, 90, 107, 108, 112, 127, 129, 130, 133, 154

Plinking 90, 118, 121

*PM* 136

Pop 16, 18, 68–70, 78, 92, 104, 105, 136

Princeton University 76

Proof house 44

Public Law 149 74

Pugsley, Edwin 43

Purdey guns 5, 64, 77, 78, 95, 146, 148, 150, 153, 158, 164

Purdey, Athol 158

Purdey, James 24, 102

Purdy, Bud 3, 21, 50, 91, 92, 158, 159, 165

Purdy, Ruth 40, 165

Q-ship 108

*Querflinte* 55

Red House 141

Red-legged partridge 158

Remington Arms 26, 82, 83

Remington, Eliphalet 41

Rhino 68, 69, 72, 78, 79, 94, 100, 104, 135

Rievaulx Abbey 62

Rifling 10, 11, 100

Rigby, John 134, 135

Robinson, Jimmy 49

Rock Island Auction 121

*Rogue* 7, 79

Roosevelt, Anna 45

Roosevelt, Eleanor 45, 154

Roosevelt, Franklin 45

Roosevelt, Theodore 6, 20, 70, 72–74, 80, 83, 84, 172

Rotary magazine 84, 86

Rothschild 87, 92, 97

Rough Riders 83

Royal Enfield 134

Russell, Jane 19

Safety catch 28, 44, 80, 105, 140, 145

San Francisco 90, 136, 146

San Francisci de Paula 65, 73

San Juan Hill 83

Sanford, P.G. 42

Santoña, Duke of 158

Sarasqueta, Victor 158

Sarezzo 62

Sauer 155

Schmeling, Max 56

Schönauer, Otto 84

Schwing, Ned 3, 16

*Scientific American* 131

Scope sight 69, 76, 77, 79, 80, 85, 86, 89, 92, 98

Scotch Tape 92

Scott, Charles 42, 146

Scott, William Middleditch 41, 146

Seward, William W. 120, 164

Shaw & Hunter 102, 109

Shelton, Rob 3, 140, 152

Sherman Anti-Trust Act 43

Shevlin, Tommy 32, 75

Shimoni 66

Shropshire 93, 106

Sidelock action 44, 64, 158

Sighting plane 28, 54

Silver Creek 25, 39, 91, 149, 159, 165

Singapore 136

Single trigger 28, 44, 83, 86, 93, 96, 97, 106

Sino-Japanese War 136

Slam-fire 14, 15, 35

Sloan's Sporting Goods Company 155

Smith & Wesson 122

Smith, Horace 41

Smith, L.C. 42

Smith, Pat 109, 111

Smokeless powder 34, 82, 84, 103, 104, 134, 135

Smoothbore 10

Softnose bullet 5

Solid bullet 5, 108, 118, 138

Sotolongo, Roberto Herrera 31, 67

*Sovrapposto* 63, 64

Spanish-American War 83

Speed, Jon 3, 137

Spiegel, Clara 40, 49, 92

Splinter forend 43

Sporterizing 74

Sportsmen's Club of Cincinnati 142

SS *Africa* 66

SS *Flandre* 120

SS *Matsona* 136

SSG 13

St. Etienne 63

St. Valentine's Day Massacre 132

Sten gun 17

Steyr 84, 91

Stiennon, Louis 43

Stoeger 138

Strater, Henry ("Mike") 16, 30, 34, 68, 69, 102, 112, 134, 138, 144

Suhl 54, 56, 57, 154, 155

Sun Valley 7, 12, 19, 20, 23, 29, 32, 33, 36–41, 46, 47, 49, 50, 77, 83, 90, 159, 162

Sutherland, Jim 94, 96, 100

Sweet 16 35, 37, 164

Take-down mechanism 88, 89, 91, 97, 123

Tanganyika 4, 70, 92, 98, 111

Tariff Act of 1883 43

Taylor, John 138

Taylor, Leslie B. 96

Tebbe, Bruce 3, 49, 50

Theisen, Earl 81, 87–89, 97, 99, 115, 116, 124, 128, 129

Thompson, Charles 70, 108, 130, 138, 139, 156

Thompson, Gen. John T. 131, 132, 133

Thumb lever 43, 98, 146

*Time* 51

Tito, Marshall 56

*Toronto Star, The* 30

Trevallion, David 3, 117, 151

Treviso 105

Trieste 150

*True* 7, 164

*True at First Light* 6, 7, 18, 70, 80, 87, 114, 115

Tsavo 136

Tumbler 64, 148

Tunney, Gene 124

U-boat 94, 107, 108, 133, 154

Udet, Ernst 98

Udine 5, 60, 140, 150

Ugartechea 22, 160

*Under Kilimanjaro* 5, 6, 7, 17, 18, 50, 59, 70, 80, 87, 105, 109, 112, 114, 115, 128, 140

Urriola, J.M. 158

Ustinov, Dmitri 34

Val Trompia 60–64, 154

Van Guilder, Gene 29, 40, 161

Venice 60–63, 66, 141, 150, 160

Ventosilla 158

Vieille, Paul 134

*Vierling* 55

*Vogue* 6, 7

Volcanic Arms Company 41

Waffen-Loesche 58

Wakamba 114

Walther 155

Warren, Walter 30

Washington, DC 136, 154

Webley & Scott 148

*Wender* 55

Wesson, Daniel 41

West, Adam 153

Western Cartridge Company 45

Westley Richards, William 96, 146

Wheel-lock 55

Whelen, Col. Townsend 69, 76

White hunter 6, 9, 16, 70, 100, 134

White, Stewart Edward 72

Whitney, Eli 41

Williams, Taylor 12, 40, 47, 60, 77, 162

Wilson, R.L. 60

Wilson, Robert 134

Winchester Model 70 92, 162, 164

Winchester, Oliver 41, 135

Winchester, Sarah 42

Woodward, James 24

Wyoming 6, 38, 46, 49, 70, 75, 77, 82, 84, 128, 156, 157

Zaphiro, Denis 18, 66, 79, 80, 81, 87, 97, 102, 109–112, 120, 129, 143

Zella-Mehlis 155